VANITY PLATE

Expressions

WALLACE DUNN

outskirts
press

Outskirts Press, Inc.
http://www.outskirtspress.com

ISBN: 978-1-4787-8384-8

Outskirts Press and the "OP" logo are trademarks belonging to Outskirts Press, Inc.

PRINTED IN THE UNITED STATES OF AMERICA

WASHINGTON

WADEE

EVERGREEN STATE

TABLE OF CONTENTS

"NUMBERS"

"LETTERS"

"A"

ALLISOK	ALL IS OK
ALLIZOK	ALL IS OK
ALTHTYM	ALL THE TIME
ALNYTLG	ALL NIGHT LONG
ABORTIT	ABORT IT
AL4U2DO	ALL FOR YOU TO DO
AL4U2DU	ALL FOR YOU TO DO
AL4YUTO	ALL FOR YOU TOO
ALL4U2	ALL FOR YOU TOO
ALL4U2B	ALL FOR YOU TO BE
ALL4U2C	ALL FOR YOU TO SEE
ALLISG	ALL IS GO
ALLIZGO	ALL IS GO
ACT4ME	ACT FOR ME
ALMYLUV	ALL MY LOVE
ALTHWAY	ALL THE WAY
AL414AL	ALL FOR ONE, ONE FOR ALL

ACT4ME2	ACT FOR ME TOO
AIS1ST	A IS FIRST
AWACNBX	AS WELL AS CAN BE EXPECTED
AWACBXD	AS WELL AS CAN BE EXPECTED
ABUZME	ABUSE ME
ABUZME2	ABUSE ME TOO
ANTQDLR	ANTIQUE DEALER
ASITWUR	AS IT WERE
AZITWUR	AS IT WERE
ASITWER	AS IT WERE
ATEBALZ	EIGHT BALLS
ALISKO	ALL IS KNOCKOUT
ALIZKO	AL IS KNOCKOUT
ALINFUN	ALL IS FUN
AQUANTZ	AQUANAUTS
ALLYUIZ	ALL YOU IS
ALLYUIS	ALL YOU IS
AZITWUZ	AS IT WAS
ASITWUZ	AS IT WAS
ALWSTUP	ALL WASHED UP
AWSHTUP	AW SHUT UP
AYE2ZEE	A TO Z
ATWOZ	A TO Z
ADACLOK	EIGHT OCLOCK
ALLOFIT	ALL OF IT
ALLASB4	ALL AS BEFORE
ALLAZB4	ALL AS BEFORE
AX2GRND	AX TO GRIND

VANITY PLATE EXPRESSIONS

ALISWEL	AL IS WELL
ALIZWEL	AL IS WELL
AZLUVLY	AS LOVELY
ALL4ZOK	ALL FOURS OK
ALBLTUP	ALL BLOWED UP
ALBLTUP	ALL BUILT UP
ARNDWLD	AROUND WORLD
ATLASIS	ATLAS IS
ATLASIZ	ATLAS IS
AZUGLY	AS UGLY
ASUGLY2	AS UGLY TOO
ARMNLEG	ARM AND LEG
ALURZ	ALLURES
ALURZME	ALLURES ME
ALABVBD	ALL ABOVE BOARD
ALLNTYM	ALL IN TIME
ASOOGLY	AS UGLY
ACUMBAC	A COMEBACK
ALCNTRY	ALL COUNTRY
ATCELVL	AT SEA LEVEL
ATSELVL	AT SEA LEVEL
ATCLEVL	AT SEA LEVEL
ACZRWLD	ACRES ARE WILD
ALLFYN	ALL FINE
ALLFINE	ALL FINE
ALZFYN	ALLS FINE
ALZFINE	ALLS FINE
ALSFYN	ALLS FINE

ALZWELL	ALLS WELL
AMBISHN	AMBITION
ATEBALS	8 BALLS
ATEBALL	8 BALL
ATEBALZ	8 BALLS
ABATEME	ABATE ME
ALLSHOT	ALL SHOT
ALIGATR	ALLIGATOR
ATEBYAL	ATE BY ALL
ABLBDYD	ABLE BODIED
ACOSTME	ACOST ME
ACQNTNZ	ACQUANTANCE
ALTURKED	ALL TUCKERED
ALLINIT	ALL IN IT
ASYSTU2	ASSIST YOU TOO
ABT2BME	ABOUT TO BE ME
ALINADA	ALL IN A DAY
ALL4U2	ALL FOR YOU TOO
AMAYZNG	AMAZING
ANEOKLE	ANNIE OAKLEY
ALL4U	ALL FOR YOU
ALL4YU	ALL FOR YOU
ASARULE	AS A RULE
AZARULE	AS A RULE
ALSMYN	ALS MINE
ALZMINE	ALS MINE
ALLUIS	ALL YOU IS
ALLUIZ	ALL YOU IS

ALLYUIS	ALL YOU IS
ALLYUIZ	ALL YOU IS
A4DABUL	AFFORDABLE
A4DABIL	AFFORDABLE
AMESSUR	A MESS YOU ARE
AMESYUR	A MESS YOU ARE
ADDITUP	ADD IT UP
ABTTYM	ABOUT TIME
ALABTME	ALL ABOUT ME
ALGSTUP	ALL GASSED UP
AL4YRLV	ALL FOR YOUR LOVE
ARDVARC	ARDVAARK
ANSRME	ANSWER ME
ANSRME2	ANSWER ME TOO
ALLNALL	ALL IN ALL
ACCENTZ	ACCENTS
ALLUVRS	ALL LOVERS
ALLVRZR	ALL LOVERS ARE
AVEONYX	AVIONICS
AVEONIX	AVIONICX
AL4BETR	ALL FOR BETTER
ALACKOF	A LACK OF
ALACKOV	A LACK OF
AGREABL	AGREEABLE
ALLLOVE	ALL LOVE
ACNOWLG	ACKNOWLEDGE
ALMYLYF	ALL MY LIFE
ALLBOYS	ALL BOYS

ALLBOYZ	ALL BOYS
AQTPROB	A CUTE PROBLEM
AQTSIS	A CUTE SISTER
ALMIXT	ALL MIXED
ATUBEST`	AT YOU BEST
ANSO4TH	AND SOFORTH
ALBDRND	ALL BE DARNED
ADITUP2	ADD IT UP TOO
AGNSTME	AGINST ME
ATUBEST	AT YOU BEST
AL4MONY	ALL FOR MONEY
ADIT4ME	ADD IT FOR ME
ABT2BME	ABOUT TO BE ME
AL4FREE	ALL FOR FREE
ALKSLZR	ALKA SELZER
ABT2BUS	ABOUT TO BE US
AZYUWER	AS YOU WERE
AIRBLOZ	AIR BLOWS
ADOREME	ADORE ME
ALYBYZ	ALIBIS
ALMYLUV	ALL MY LOVE
ANNOD	DONNA BACKWARDS
ADOORME	ADORE ME
AVOYDME	AVOID ME
ARABRAB	BARBARA BACKWARDS
ATURNEE	ATTORNEY
A4RDIT	AFFORD IT
A4RDIT2	AFFORD IT TOO

VANITY PLATE EXPRESSIONS

ATOYOTA	A TOYOTA BACKWADS
ATEBFOR	ATE BEFORE
ATEB4YU	ATE BEFORE YOU
AWRYTGO	AWE RIGHT GO
ALISAIR	ALL IS AIR
ALIZAIR	ALL IS AIR
ALABTYU	ALL ABOUT YOU
ALBUTU	ALL BUT YOU
ALBUTYU	ALL BUT YOU
ACNTENT	ACCOUNTANT
ANGLAFAC	ANGLEFACE
ALPDFOR	ALL PAID FOR
ALPD4	ALL PAID FOR
ALPAID4	ALL PAID FOR
ALL4FUN	ALL FOR FUN
APLSTDL	APPLE STRUDEL
ALLTURD	ALTERED
AWRT4U	AWE RIGHT FOR YOU
AWRT4Y	AWE RIGHT FOR YOU
ACCT4IT	ACCOUNT FOR IT
ALLBULL	ALL BULL
AFRWHCR	AFTER WHILE CROCIDLE
ANGLZDO	ANGLES DO
ANGLZDU	ANGLES DO
ANSRSNO	ANSWERS NO
ABALONE	ABALONE SEAFOOD
ACHINFT	ACHIN FEET
AROBICS	AROBICS

ASALTED	ASSUALTED
AWDRYUP	AWE DRY UP
AWDRIUP	AWE DRY UP
ABACUS	COUNTING BOARD
ABDUCTR	ABDUCTOR
ABDUCKT	ABDUCT
ARELBOR	A REAL BORE
AKSENTZ	ACCENTS
AKCENTS	ACCENTS
AKCENTZ	ACCENTS
AKSENTS	ACCENTS
ACSESRY	ACCESSORY
ACTSTRG	ACT STRANGE
AQZERZ	ACCUSERS
AQZURZ	ACCUSERS
AQZERS	ACCUSERS
ACEHIGH	ACE HIGH
ACNHOLE	ACE IN HOLE
ACUSTIX	ACCOUSTICS
ADANNEV	ADAM AN EVE
ACTUATE	TO PUT IN MOTION
ACTU8	ACTUATE
ACTU8ED	ACTUATED
ACUTE1	A CUTE ONE
ADAGIO	SLOW AND LIESURELY
ADAMENT	NOT GIVING UP
ADMIRED	A DELIGHT
ADOBEJO	NICKNAME

ADUNCKT	CURVING INWARD
AIRBORN	HIGH
AFILI8T	AFFILIATE
AFFIXME	JOINED TOGETHER
A4THOT	AFORE THOUGHT
A4TIME	TIMES NOW PAST
AFREET	EVIL DEMON
AFTRHRS	AFTER HOURS
AFTRHRZ	AFTER HOURS
AGIT8TD	AGITATED
AGIT8TD	AGITATED
AGOKNEE	AGONY
AGAKNEE	AGONY
ALIEN8T	ALIENATED
ALOITH	BIG DIPPER STAR
ALEGENZ	ALLEGIANCE
AMORIST	OCCUPIED IN LOVEMAKING
ACFTPLT	AIRCRAFT PILOT
ACFTOPR	AIRCRAFT OPERATOR
ACFTDVR	AIRCRAFT DRIVER
AVASHUN	AVIATION
AV8TOR	AVIATOR
AV8TORE	AVIATOR
ASKISSR	AS KISSER
ASKISR	AS KISSER
ASKICKR	AS KICKER
ALIGTRZ	ALLIGATORS
ALGRTRZ	ALLIGATOR TEARS

ALL4ME2	ALL FOR ME TOO
ALFABET	ALPHABET
ANNAHYM	ANAHEIM, CALIF
ATLBRVS	ATLANTA BRAVES
AFTERU	AFTER YOU
AFTERYU	AFTER YOU
AMATOUR	AMATEUR
ANALYZE	ANALYZE
ATTACKT	ATTACKED
AROBICS	AROBICS
AROBIKS	AROBICS
AROBIX	AROBICS
AROBIKS	AROBICS
AIRLOOM	HEIRLOOM
AIRLUME	HEIRLOOM
ALFALFA	ALFALFA
ANTETER	ANTEATER
ACROBAT	ACROBAT
AGAZNOG	GONZAGA BACKWARDS
ALOYOL	LOYOLA BACKWARDS
AYRBOTE	AIRBOAT
ATHEBZR	AT THE BUZZER
ALL4ME2	ALL FOR ME TOO
ABTYME	ABOUT TIME
ABTTYME	ABOUT TIME
ABTTIME	ABOUT TIME
AKTZOVR	ACTS OVER
ACTZOVR	ACTS OVER

AWHOLE	A WHOLE
ALTUNA	CITY IN PA.
ALKITRZ	ISLAND IN CALIF.
ASTRNOT	ASTRONAUT
AFTERYU	AFTER YOU
AFTERU	A AFTER YOU
ASKME2	ASK ME TOO
ASKME2C	ASK ME TO SEE
ALLNFUN	ALL IN FUN
AYNITIT	AIN'T IT IT
ASPR8ED	ASPIRATED
AHACOTU	AHA CAUGHT YOU
ALWYSLT	ALWAYS LIT
ALCRKTU	ALL CRACKED UP
AYRFLYT	AIR FLIGHT
ARNTUQT	AREN'T YOU CUTE
ASKME2	ASK ME TOO
ASKME2C	ASK ME TO SEE
ASAPPLZ	AS SOON AS POSSIBLE PLEASE
ASAPLZ	AS SOON AS POSSIBLE PLEASE
A10DENT	ATTENDANT
ASSFALT	ASPHALT
A10SHUN	ATTENTION
ALIBYZ	ALIBIS
ARMZHUT	ARMEN TO HILT
AIRFUR8	AIR FREIGHT
ASPRGUS	ASPARAGUS
ASKMETO	ASK ME TOO

ASKME2	ASK ME TOO
ASKME1	ASK ME ONE
ASKME41	ASK ME FOR ONE
ASKME42	ASK ME FOR TOO
AWLB4YU	ALL BEFORE YOU
ARABRAB	BARBARA BACKWARDS

"B"

BURDZDU	BIRDS DO
BIRDZDU	BIRDS DO
BENAXT	BEEN AXED
BEDLAM	BEDLAM
BUTRFLY	BUTTERFLY
BLKBYRD	BLACK BIRD
BLUBIRD	BLUE BIRD
BLUBYRD	BLUE BIRD
BUZZARD	BUZZARD
BACROWD	BACK ROAD
BIGPUBA	BIG BOSS
BESWEET	BE SWEET
BESUITE	BE SWEET
BSIRIUS	BE SERIOUS
BAGUDGY	BE A GOOD GUY
BAWINR	BE A WINNER
BEMASIVE	BE MASSIVE

BAMESS	BE A MESS
BETRBUZ	BETTER BOOZE
BEERZOK	BEERS OK
BIZEBE	BUZY BEE
BUTIFUL	BEAUTIFUL
BTFULIZ	BEAUTIFUL IS
BTFLIZ	BEAUTIFUL IS
BTFLBDY	BEAUTIFUL BODY
BCREWL	BE CREUL
BUCKSAW	BUCKSAW
BIGCHEF	BIG CHEF
BIZ4BOY	B IS FOR BOY
BHEADER	BEHEADER
BETSYJO	BETSY JO
BETCJO	BETSY JO
BETCJOE	BETSY JOE
BULLDOG	BULLDOG
BADINFO	BAD INFORMATION
BUGEZOK	BOOGIES OK
BYMEIT	BUY ME IT
BUYMEIT	BUY ME IT
BEITSO	BE IT SO
BEEITSO	BE IT SO
BITSO	BE IT SO
BADBRKS	BAD BREAKS
B4UDUIT	BEFORE YOU DO IT
BIRDSDO	BIRDS DO
BIS4BOO	B IS FOR BOO

BYDFALT	BY DEFAULT
B4UDOIT	BEFORE YOU DO IT
BIRDSDU	BIRDS DO
BURDSDU	BIRDS DO
BYOBPLZ	BRING YOUR OWN BOOZE PLEASE
BITEIT2	BITE IT 2
BYRETAL	BUY RETAIL
B4ULEAP	BEFORE YOU LEAP
BIRDDUE	BIRD DOO
BYOBRTO	BRING YOUR OWN BURRITO
BYTIT	BITE IT
BYHOLSL	BUY WHOLESALE
B42LATE	BEFORE TOO LATE
BIGDUDE	BIG DUDE
BYTIT2	BITE IT TOO
BYBYGRZ	BUY BY GROSS
BYBYGRS	BUY BY GROSS
BARECUB	BEAR CUB
BIGDUD	BIG DUD
B4ULVME	BEFORE YOU LEAVE ME
BLOZITZ	BLOWS ITS
BEQUIK	BE QUICK
BQUIK	BE QUICK
BEEQUICK	BE QUICK
BIGGUY	BIG GUY
BITRSWT	BITTER SWEET
BTRSWET	BITTER SWEET
BTRSWT	BITTER SWEET

BARZBST	BARS BEST
BYME12	BUY ME ONE TOO
BAGABON	BAGABON
BOTFARM	BOUGHT FARM
BTRU2ME	BE TRUE TO ME
BUYME12	BUY ME ONE TOO
BAGABNZ	BAG A BONES
BADNOOS	BAD NEWS
BADNOOZ	BAD NEWS
BADNEWS	BAD NEWS
BEGOOD2	BE GOOD TOO
BGOOD2	BE GOOD TOO
BADZBAD	BADS BAD
BIGTULZ	BIG TOOLS
BARWITZ	BARE WITS
BADNEWZ	BAD NEWS
BLUZKUL	BLUES COOL
BLOHARD	BLOW HARD
BRAYNPR	BRAIN POWER
BRWITME	BEAR WITH ME
BEVIZOK	BEV IS OK
BEVISOK	BEV IS OK
BORDONE	BORED ONE
BOTMZUP	BOTTOMS UP
BOTMSUP	BOTTOMS UP
BALDZIN	BALDS IN
BALDSIN	BALDS IN
BONISOK	BONNIE IS OK

BONIZOK	BONNIE IS OK
BEITSO	BE IT SO
BITSO	BE IT SO
BEITSEW	BE IT SO
BORD1	BORED ONE
BOARD1	BORED ONE
BORDONE	BORAD ONE
BRUSEME	BRUISE ME
BRUZEME	BUISE ME
BORN2B1	BORN TO BE ONE
BITMAY	BE IT MAY
BEITMAY	BE IT MAY
BSYRIUS	BE SERIOUS
BORN2BE	BORN TO BE
BRUZME	BRUISE ME
BSYREUS	BE SERIOUS
B4YULV	BEFORE YOU LEAVE
B4UCME	BEFORE YOU SEE ME
B4U2CME	BEFORE YOU TOO SEE ME
BORNFRE	BORN FREE
BADDAYZ	BAD DAYS
BADDAZE	BAD DAYS
BANDAYD	BAND AID
BIZEBEE	BUSY BEE
BUGOFF	BUG OFF
BURPZUP	BURPS UP
BURPSUP	BURPS UP
BIZEBEZ	BUSY BEE

B42LATE	BEFORE TOO LATE
BETMETO	BET ME TOO
BETME4U	BET ME FOR YOU
BETME42	BET ME FOR TWO
BARK4ME	BARK FOR ME
BORZME2	BORES ME TOO
BITEIT2	BITE IT TOO
BORDBE4	BORED BEFORE
BUSTME	BUST ME
BUSTME2	BUST ME TOO
BETME2	BET ME TOO
BYSYKO	BICYCLE
BYSICO	BICYCLE
BISYKO	BICYCLE
BISICO	BICYCLE
BADNSAD	BAD AN SAD
BURYMYA	BURY MY A**
BALZNAL	BALLS N ALL
BALSNAL	BALLS N ALL
BABYLUV	BABY LOVE
BEARDWN	BARE DOWN
BAREDWN	BARE DOWN
BALMEOT	BALL ME OUT
BLZAFYR	BALLS A FIRE
BLKNBLU	BLACK N BLUE
BATHEME	BATHE ME
BEWINR	BE A WINNER
BAWYNR	BE A WINNER

BAWIMP	BE A WIMP
BRTSTAR	BRIGHT STAR
BRYTSTR	BRIGHT STAR
BMYBUDY	BE MY BUDDY
BRASTAX	BRASS TACKS
BLUDZRD	BLOODS RED
BLUBLUD	BLUE BLOOD
BAWINR	BE A WINNER
BMYBDY	BE MY BUDDY
BMYBUDY	BE MY BUDDY
BMYBODY	BE MY BUDDY
BRAZTAX	BRASS TRACKS
BLUEZBLUE	BLUES BLUE
BENDUPT	BEENDUPED
BABYCRY	BABY CRY
BYTYURT	BITE YOUR TONGUE
BYTUTNG	BITE YOUR TONGUE
BORN2B	BORN TO BE
BORN2BE	BORN TO BE
BUZEIT	BOOZE IT
BOOKWRM	BOOKWORM
BUGSROK	BUGS ARE OK
BUGZROK	BUGS ARE OK
BYTYURZ	BITE YOURS
BURNZME	BURNS ME
BUZEIT2	BOOZE IT TOO
BYFRNOW	BYE FOR NOW
BYFURNW	BY FOR NOW

BYE4NOW	BYE FOR NOW
BADMOVE	BAD MOVE
BADMOOV	BAD MOVE
BERNME	BURN ME
BURNMYN	BURN MINE
B1B4UGO	BE ONE BEFORE YOU GO
BETRB1	BETTER BE ONE
BETRB12	BETTER BE ONE TOO
BETRBSW	BETTER BE SWEET
B4UCALL	BEFORE YOU CALL
BECREWL	BE CRUEL
BUTZRIN	BUTTS ARE IN
BSKTKAS	BASKET CASE
BAGABLZ	BAG A BLUES
BNSUCRD	BEEN SUCKERED
BEZWAXZ	BEEN WAX
BNYC2ME	BE NICE TO ME
BHON2ME	BE HONEST TO ME
BIGEYES	BIG EYES
BIGIZ	BIG EYES
BULLEME	BULLY ME
BYBY4ME	BYEBYE FOR ME
BACKPAX	BACK PACKS
BIGEYEZ	BIG EYES
BLOWOUT	BLOWOUT
BVRPOND	BEAVER POND
BYZROD	BUSY ROAD
B1B4UDO	BE ONE BEFORE YOU DO

BRMCHRM	BEDROOM CHARM
BATLAX	BATTLE AXE
BATLAXE	BATTLE AXE
BLKZBLK	BLACKS BLACK
BDSKYZD	BE DISGUISED
BELTME1	BELT ME ONE
BELTME2	BELT ME TOO
BUBLEZ	BUBBLES
BUBBLEZ	BUBBLES
BUBBLES	BUBBLES
BALASHZ	BALLET SHOES
BUTEME	BOOT ME
BOOTME	BOOT ME
BOOTME1	BOOT ME ONE
BOOTME2	BOOT ME TOO
BUBUSTR	BUBBIE BUSTER
BRNTHOT	BRILLIANT THOUGHT
BURNTUP	BURNED UP
BRNTOST	BURNED TOAST
B4UDROP	BEFORE YOU DROP
BIGBUKS	BIG BUCKS
BIGBUX	BIG BUCKS
BIGBUCZ	BIG BUCKS
BIGBUKZ	BIG BUCKS
BABYDOL	BABY DOLL
BAYBDOL	BABY DOLL
BYHOSAL	BUY WHOLESALE
BPURFCT	BE PERFECT

BUFSTYL	BUFF STYLE
BMYLYF	BE MY LIFE
BMYLYFE	BE MY LIFE
BMYLUV	BE MY LOVE
BMYLOVE	BE MY LOVE
BKND2ME	BE KIND TO ME
BARBEQ	BARBEQUE
BARBQ	BARBEQUE
BARSKYN	BEAR SKIN
BRTSNRZ	BRIGHT SUNRISE
BNCRSHR	BONECRUSHER (CHIROPRACTOR)
BSTINGR	BEE STINGE
BUTRCLM	BUTTERCLAM
BRNACLE	BARNACLE
BATHZ42	BATHS FOR TWO
BLKVLVT	BLACK VELVET
BVELVET	BLACK VELVET
B4ULVME	BEFOR YOU LEAVE ME
B4UGO2	BEFORE YOU GO TO
B4UGOTO	BEFORE YOU GO TO
BETUCAN	BET YOU CAN
BETUKEN	BET YOU CAN
BYORSLF	BE YOURSELF
BOBESOX	BOBBIE SOCKS
BOBSOXR	BOBBIE SOCKS
B4UGO	BEFORE YOU GO
B4UGLO	BEFORE YOU GO

BRDNBTR	BREAD N BUTTER
BURYME2	BURY ME TOO
BEEQUIK	BE QUICK
BQUIK	BE QUICK
BEQUICK	BE QUICK
BUMRAP	BUM RAP
BUMBRAP	BUM RAP
BUMRAPT	BUM RAPPED
B4UFLIP	BEFORE YOU FLIP
BATOPER	BE A TOPER
BATOPR	BE A TOPER
B4UGO2H	BEFORE YOU GO TO HEAVEN
BMYBEST	BE MY BEST
BURBEST	BE YOUR BEST
BUNYHOP	BUNNY HOP
BABUNGY	BE A BUN GUY
BUZ4YU	BUNS FOR YOU
BUNZ4U	BUNS FOR YOU
BLYDNCR	BELLY DANCER
BELYDNR	BELLY DANCER
BAYKUR	BAKER
BARBURR	BARBER
BLKSMIT	BLACKSMITH
BKBINDR	BOOKBINDER
BREWER	BREWER
BRKLAYR	BRICKLAYER
BUTCHER	BUTCHER
BUSDRVR	BUS DRIVER

BADGERD	BADGERED
BUBLING	BUBBLING
BACKFYR	BACK FIRE
BUTRCUP	BUTTERCUP
BOWLER	BOWLER
BROWNIE	BROWNIE
BTRSCTC	BUTTERSCOTCH
BTRSCOT	BUTTERSCOTCH
BTRDRUM	BUTTERED RUM
BLOITUP	BLOW IT UP
BUTFULL	BEAUTIFUL
BOWLONE	BOWL ONE
BEETME	BEAT ME
BSIDESU	BESIDES YOU
BSIDEYU	BESIDE YOU
BSYDYU	BESIDE YOU
BSIGHDU	BESIDE YOU
BHONEST	BE HONEST
BTRU2ME	BE TRUE TO ME
BROKEIT	BROKE IT
BETYRAS	BET YOU'RE A**
BARFLYZ	BARFLIES
BKNOTTY	BE NAUGHTY
BNTY4ME	BE NAUGHTY FOR ME
BDYPNTG	BODY PAINTING
BENT2HE	BENT TO HELL
BENT2HL	BENT TO HELL
BENT2H	BENT TO HELL

BENROBD	BEEN BOBBED
BMYGEST	BE MY GUEST
BUTUGLY	BUT UGLY
BUMONRN	BUMMIN ROUND
BUMNRND	BUMMIN ROUND
BNCBACK	BOUNCE BACK
BOWNCBK	BOUNCE BACK
BLBRMOU	BLABBER MOUTH
BLOWGUN	BLOWGUN
BLOGUNR	BLOWGUNNER
BY1GT1F	BUY ONE GET ONE FREE
BKEYPUR	BOOKKEEPER
BKKEPR	BOOKKEEPER
BABABLS	BABA BLACK SHEEP
BBSITTR	BABYSITTER
BAYBSTR	BABYSITTER
BAYBSIT	BABYSIT
BEDBUGZ	BEDBUGS
BODYODR	BODY ODOR
BODEODR	BODY ODER
BLAKJAC	BLACK JACK
BLACJAC	BLACK JACK
BLINDTZ	BLIND DATES
BINGO	BINGO
BINGOE	BINGO
BKEYPER	BEEKEEPER
BKEYPUR	BEEKEEPER
BONSAI	BONSAI

BUMRANG	BOOMERRANG
BUMRING	BUM RING
BRKNBNZ	BRODEN BONES
BEFSTKE	BEEF STEAK
BFSTAKE	BEEF STEAK
BROCLI	BROCCOLI
BROCKLE	BROCCOLI
BROKLEE	BROCCOLI
BROKLEIT	BROCCOLI
BUCKSAW	BUCKSAW
BYOBODY	BRING YOUR OWN BODY
BLKBOTM	BLACK BOTTOM
BUGMEPZ	BUG ME PLEASE
BUGMEPL	BUG ME PLEASE
BGMEPLZ	BUG ME PLEASE
BACLASH	BACKLASH
BAKLASH	BACKLASH
BOYRUQT	BOY ARE YOU CUTE
BOYURQT	BOY ARE YOU CUTE
BUGKILR	BUG KILLER
BUGLIKR	BUG LICKER
BUGLICR	BUG LICKER
BUGWACR	BUG WACKER
BUGWAKR	BUG WACKER
BXLUNCH	BOX LUNCH
BIGHUTRZ	BIG HOOTERS
BTNSHUZ	BUTTON SHOES
BTNURLP	BUTTON YOUR LIP

BAGGITT	BAG IT
BRZBEST	BEERS BEST
BERZBST	BEERS BEST
BZYMYND	BUSY MIND
BSYMIND	BUSY MIND
BYADUCK	BUY A DUCK
BOOKTUP	BOOKED UP
BYMYTYM	BY MY TIME
BIGQBZ	BIG CUBES
BIGNBAD	BIG AN BAD
BADLOSR	BAD LOSER
BADLUZR	BAD LOSER
BADLOZR	BAD LOSER
BADAPLZ	BAD APPLES
BADAPLS	BAD APPLES
BLASTED	BLASTED
BLASTER	BLASTER
BLUEBERD	BLUE BIRD
BLUJAYZ	BLUE JAYS
BLUJAYS	BLUE JAYS
BOSRDSX	BOSTON RED SOX
BADANSR	BAD ANSWER
BUTNBTN	BUTTON BUTTON
BKOFFJK	BACK OFF JACK
BAYSBAL	BASEBALL
BAYZBAL	BASEBALL
BARKS2	BARKS TOO
BARKZ2	BARKS TOO

BAWLZ2	BALLS TOO
BUTRNUT	BUTTERNUT
BANKROL	BANDROLL
BAWL4ME	BALL FOR ME
BUZZ4ME	BUZZ FOR ME
BANJO	BANJO
BANJOE	BANJO
BEDROLE	BEDROLL
BEDROLL	BEDROLL
BREEZIE	BREEZIE
BACNBGR	BACONBURGER
BAYGELL	BAGEL
BURRGER	BURGER
BIGBOPR	BIG BOPPER
BYTHELB	BY THE POUND
BITTERN	BITTERN (BIRD)
BTWXBWN	BETWIX N BETWEEN
BAKHAND	BACKHAND
BACHAND	BACKHAND
B42LONG	BEFORE TOO LONG
BUFALOW	BUFFALO
BOSSTUN	BOSTON, MA
BEARCLA	BEARCLAW
BEARCLW	BEARCLAW
BRDWALK	BOARDWALK
BCUZUR	BECAUSE YOU ARE
BCUZUAR	BECAUSE YOU ARE
BTBURBT	BUTT BUSTER

BSTURBT	BUST YOUR BUTT
BRAINSG	BRAIN SURGEON
BYAHAIR	BY A HAIR
BSWT2ME	BE SWEET TO ME
BTUGLY2	BUT UGLY TOO
BUTUGLY	BUT UGLY
BATLEAX	BATTLE AXE
BDYMVMT	BODY MOVEMENT
BCUZUQT	BECAUSE YOUR QUIET
BSHWACR	BUSH WHACKER
BSHWAKR	BUSH WHACKER
BYTHEHR	BY THE HOUR
BUCKLUP	BUCKLE UP
BNCHCRP	BUNCH CRAP
BNCACRP	BUNCH A CRAP
BRN2SH	BORN TO SHOP
BRD2DE	BORED TO DEATH
BOWTOUW	BOW TO U.W.
BOW2UW	BOW TO U.W.
BACHLRS	BATCHELORS DEGREE
BACHLRZ	BATCHELORS DEGREE
BISICLE	BICYCLE
BISICLZ	BICYCLES
BYSICLZ	BICYCLES
BIGHTME	BITE ME
BITEME2	BITE ME TOO
BUXSTOP	BUCKS STOP
BYALMNS	BY ALL MEANS

BYALMNZ	BY ALL MEANS
BULDOZR	BULLDOZER
BLUDZRD	BLOODS RED
BDIPTIN	BE DIPPED IN?
BLUEYES	BLUE EYES
BIGBUKZ	BIG BUCKS
BYGTYGR	BIG TIGER
BIGTYGR	BIG TIGER
BMYSDAD	BE MY SUGAR DADDY
BAQUEEN	BE A QUEEN
BOWWOW	REAL DOG
BBDWOLF	BIG BAD WOLF
BATTRUP	BATTER UP
BATRUP	BATTER UP
BMYGEST	BE MY GUEST
BZBUZIN	BEES BUZZIN
BMYBOOB	BE MY BOOB
BUTUGLY	BUTT UGLY
BEETZME	BEATS ME
BSIRTIN	BE CERTAIN
BESQUARE	BE SQUARE
BUNGALO	BUNGALOW
BIGBAD1	BIG BAD ONE
BTWNUS	BETWEEN US
BTWENUS	BETWEEN US
BENRECT	BEEN WRECKED
BMYBABY	BE MY BABY
BA4MAN	BE A FOREMAN

VANITY PLATE EXPRESSIONS

BPAYSNT	BE PATIENT
BTRUSTD	BE TRUSTED
BABBLER	LOOSE TONGUE
BMYBUDY	BE MY BUDDY
BELTUP	BELT UP
BEEREAL	BE REAL
BEEREEL	BE REAL
B14SURE	BE ONE FOR SURE
BAKMEUP	BACK ME UP
BAKMEIN	BACK ME IN
BTRU2ME	BE TRUE TO ME
BUMBLBZ	BUMBLE BEE
BUMBLEB	BUMBLE BEE
BRBNH2O	BOURBON AND WATERB
BYRDLVR	BIRD LOVER
BIRDLVR	BIRD LOVER
B4YUAWL	BEFOR YOU ALL
B4YUALL	BEFORE YOU ALL
BIGLUZR	BIG LOSER

"C"

CULATER	SEE YOU LATER
CREMAWH	CREAM A WHEAT
CME4LVG	SEE ME FOR LOVING
CME4LOV	SEE ME FOR LOVE
CKYMSTR	COOKIE MONSTER
COYNCOL	COIN COLLECTOR
CMEB46	SEE ME BEFORE SIX
CANIFWE	CAN IF WE
COMFYME	COMFY ME
CANIFUR	CAN IF YOU ARE
CTNPICR	COTTON PICKER
CTNPIKR	COTTON PICKER
CLEVER1	CLEVER ONE
CHWITUP	CHEW IT UP
CHOOCHU	CHOO CHOO
CHUCHOO	CHOO CHOO
CRYBABY	CRYBABY

CLKWTCR	CLOCK WATCHER
COLISHN	COLLISION
C2IT2	SEE TO IT TOO
CPYKATZ	COPY CATS
CIT4ME	SEE IT FOR ME
CUZU2R	CAUSE YOU TWO ARE
CITNOW	SEE IT NOW
CUZIDO	CAUSE I DO
CUZIDOO	CAUSE I DO
CUZIDUE	CAUSE I DO
CUZWEDO	CAUSE WE DO
CUCUZUN	SEE YOU COUSIN
CUCUZN	SEE YOU COUSIN
CANUCME	CAN YOU SEE ME
CALIKO	CALICO
CANRAC	CARNAC BACKWARDS
C2ITZMN	SEE TO ITS MINE
COOLIT	COOL IT
CULEIT	COOL IT
CMENOW	SEE ME NOW
CMELATR	SEE ME LATER
CASTME	CAST ME
CASTME2	CAST ME TOO
CATZCAN	CATS CAN
CBZROK2	CBS ARE OK TO
CBZRIN	CBS ARE IN
CRANKIT	CRANK IT
CUZIMOK	CAUSE I'M OK

CUZIM	CAUSE I AM
CARZSUC	CARS SUCK
CARSSUK	CARS SUCK
CARZSUK	CARS SUCK
CALLME2	CALL ME TOO
CROKRAP	CROCKACRAP
CANTFIX	CANT FIX
CLASACT	CLASS ACT
CNTMEIN	COUNT ME IN
CTMEIN	COUNT ME IN
CTMEIN2	COUNT ME IN TOO
CRYBABY	CRY BABY
CRYBABE	CRY BABY
CMEIFUR	SEE ME IF YOU ARE
CIFICAR	SEE IF I CARE
CIFIKAR	SEE IF I CARE
CPRZOK	C.P.R. IS OK
CPRNSTR	CPR INSTRUCTOR
CROKIT	CROK IT
CORKZIN	CORKS IN
CANUTVL	CAN YOU TRAVEL
CLOCKIT	CLOCK IT
CLOKITN	CLOCK IT IN
CRKOFDN	CRACK OF DAWN
CRKOVDN	CRACK OF DAWN
CU2NITE	SEE YOU TONIGHT
CU2NYTE	SEE YOU TONIGHT
CUMBACK	COME BACK

CVRURAS	COVER YOU'RE A**
CUTITUP	CUT IT UP
CIFUCAN	SEE IF YOU CAN
CIFICAN	SEE IF I CAN
C2IT241	SEE TO IT TO FOR ONE
CITONME	SEE IT ON ME
CYITIS	SEE WHY IT IS
CYITIZ	SEE WHY IT IS
CQUREME	SECURE ME
C2QTIZ	SEE TWO CUTE EYES
CALOREZ	CALORIES
CANUCIT	CAN YOU SEE IT
CRY4ME	CRY FOR ME
CRY4ME2	CRY FOR ME TOO
CGULSR	SEAGULLS ARE
CGULZAR	SEAGULLS ARE
CLB4UCM	CALL BEFORE YOU COME
CRAZWLD	CRAZY WILD
CIFULV	SEE IF YOU LOVE
CIFULOV	SEE IF YOU LOVE
CIFULUV	SEE IF YOU LOVE
CULOVER	SEE YOU LOVER
CU2LOVR	SEE YOU TOO LOVER
CLVZOK	SEE LOVES OK
CLVZOK2	SEE LOVES OK TOO
CLUVBUG	SEE LOVE BUG
CLVBUGZ	SEE LOVE BUGS
CUDABEN	COULD A BEEN

CUM2CME	COME TO SEE ME
CIFIDO	SEE IF I DO
COLTRKE	COLD TURKEY
CDUCED	SEDUCED
CDUCET	SEDUCED
CDUCEME	SEDUCE ME
CHRMBRD	CHAIRMAN BOARD
CHMNBRD	CHAIRMAN BOARD
CASINPT	CASE IN POINT
C14US2	SEE ONE FOR US TOO
COTUAGN	CAUGHT YOU AGAIN
COTUB4	CAUGHT YOU BEFORE
CUBBARE	CUB BEAR
CUBBEAR	CUB BEAR
CRUZNBY	CRUISIN BY
CUTMEIN	CUT ME IN
C2IT2	SEE TO IT TOO
CTMEOUT	COUNT ME OUT
CKMEOUT	CHECK ME OUT
CRACRJX	CRACKER JACKS
CRKRJAX	CRACKER JACKS
CRAKRJX	CRACKER JACKS
CRCRJAX	CRACKER JACKS
CHAWKZ	SEAHAWKS
CHWKS	SEAHAWKS
CEEATL	SEATTLE
CEEATLE	SEATTLE
CIFIDUE	SEE IF I DO

CIFICAN	SEE IF I CAN
CIFIKEN	SEE IF I CAN
CKITOUT	CHECK IT OUT
CRACKIN	CRACKIN
CRAKIN	CRACKIN
CRACKN2	CRACKIN TOO
CITYGAL	CITY GAL
CKIT4ME	CHECK IT FOR ME
CRAXRIN	CHACKS ARE IN
CNSETD1	CONCEITED ONE
CHOKMYN	CHOKE MINE
CRY4US	CRY FOR US
CHNLYNX	CHAIN LINKS
CLUMEIN	CLUE ME IN
CLMCHDR	CLAM CHOWDER
CAREUTZ	CARROTS
CANITB2	CAN IT BE TWO
CIRCLIT	CIRCLE IT
CNTMEIN	COUNT ME IN
CTMEIN2	COUNT ME IN TOO
CRBGRAS	CRABGRASS
C4URSLF	SEE FOR YOURSELF
CTRPILR	CATERPILAR
CNTAPED	CENTIPEDE
CRICKET	CRICKET
CRNSYRP	CORN SYRUP
CHECKUP	CHECK UP
CHINOOK	CHINOOK

CONDORZ	CONDORS
COBRA	COBRA
COOTER	COOTER (REPTILE)
CROKDYL	CROCODILE
CLOVRLF	CLOVER LEAF
CURUNEK	SEE YOU ARE UNIQUE
CYURUNK	SEE WHY YOU ARE UNIQUE
CUTIEPY	CUTIE PIE
CRACPOT	CRACKPOT
CRAKPOT	CRACKPOT
CRKTPOT	SYCOCERAMIC
COUCHPO	COUCH POTATO
COCHPOT	COUCH POTATO
COCHPTO	COUCH POTATO
CALORYZ	CALORIES
CRNFLKS	CORN FLAKES
CRNFLKZ	CORN FLAKES
CORNFKS	CORN FLAKES
CNACRUZ	SCENICRUISE
COCKLE	COCKLE (SEAFOOD)
CKYCUTR	COOKIE CUTTER
CHARADE	CHARADE
CLOWN	CKOWN
CHASTIZ	CHASTISE
CROSFYR	CROSS FIRE
C4ONLYU	SEE FOR ONLY YOU
CMYDAD	SEE MY DAD
CMYDADY	SEE MY DADDY

CREWSIN	CREWS IN
CREWZIN	CREWS IN
CUSUEN	SEE YOU SOON
CHUCKLE	CHUCKLE
CHUCKLZ	CHUCKLES
CHRISTL	CRYSTAL
CRYSTAL	CHRISTAL
CRAZY8Z	CRAZY EIGHTS
CRIBAGE	CRIBBAGE
CHECKRZ	CHECKERS
CHECKRS	CHECKERS
CARPNTR	CARPENTER
COBBLER	COBBLER
CHEERY	CHERRY
CHEETAH	CHEETAH
COMPUTR	COMPUTER
COTNGYN	COTTON GIN
CALQLUS	CALCULUS
CUNSULT	CONSULT
CLIMBER	CLIMBER
CCLER	CYCLER
CAMBUFF	CAMERA BUFF
CARREX	CAR WRECKS
CARRECX	CAR WRECKS
CARINSR	CAR INSURANCE
COWPOKE	COWPOKE
COWPOLK	COWPOKE
CMYLOGO	SEE MY LOGO

CLASCLN	CLASS CLOWN
CHAIRIE	CHERRY
CRAZTYM	CRAZY TIMES
CULTRAL	SEE YOU LATER ALLIGATOR
CUOWNLY	SEE YOU ONLY
CONLYU	SEE ONLY YOU
CMYFIGR	SEE MY FIGURE
CMYFNGR	SEE MY FINGER
CPTCRPR	CARPET CREEPER
CRCDSHP	CREDIT CARD SHOPPER
CRCDSHR	CREDIT CARD SHOPPER
CRCDLVR	CREDIT CARD LOVER
CHARADS	CHARADES
CHICKRS	CHINESE CHECKERS
CHICKRZ	CHINESE CHECKERS
CHOPSTX	CHOP STICKS
CRCTBKR	CIRCUIT BREAKER
CLAMBKZ	CLAMBAKES
CLAMDUP	CLAMMED UP
CROQUET	CROQUET
CRCOSKI	CROSS COUNTRY SKIING
CABBAGE	CABBAGE
CMOFCHN	CREAM OF CHICKEN
CROFCHN	CREAM OF CHICKEN
CROFCKN	CREAM OF CHICKEN
CROFMSM	CREAM OF MUSHROOM
CRAZLUK	CRAZY LUCK
CHEATIN	CHEATIN

CNTLOPE	CANTALOPE
CANASTA	CANASTA
CANUING	CANOEING
CTRPLRZ	CATERPILLARS
CENTPDZ	CENTIPEDES
CHOWYUK	CHINESE FOOD
CHICKAD	CHICKADEE
CHEPTHL	CHEAP THRILL
CRZYLGZ	CRAZY LEGS
CMEWOK	SEE ME WALK
CMYWOK	SEE MY WALK
CUM2ME	COME TO ME
CUINCRT	SEE YOU IN COURT
CONDOKD	CONDO KID
CAT9LIF	CAT NINE LIVES
CAT9LYF	CAT NINE LIVES
CCZRESP	CREDIT CARDS ARE EXPENSIVE
CCZRXPS	CREDIT CARDS ARE EXPENSIVE
CRNHSKR	UNIV. OF NABRASKA
CANGELS	CALIFORNIA ANGELS
CHIWTSX	CHICAGO WHITE SOX
CINREDS	CINCINNATI REDS
CINREDZ	CINCINNATI REDS
COUGHE	COFFEE
COMINON	COMING ON
CKGACCT	CHECKING ACCOUNT
COFEPOT	COFFEEPOT
CLERICE	CLEAR ICE

CROBIN	SEE ROBIN
CHKMATE	CHECKMATE
CTRMOVE	COUNTER MOVE
CATCHUP	CATSUP
CHEDHER	CHEDDAR
CHATTER	CHATTER
CHATRBOX	CHATTERBOX
CHIRP4U	CHIRP FOR YOU
CORNBEF	CORN BEEF
CRNBEEF	CORN BEEF
CRNECGEZ	CREAM CHEESE
CHIRPZ2	CHIRPS TOO
CROWZ2	CROWS TOO
CLIFHGR	CLIFF HANGAR
CQUOUT2	SEEK YOU OUT TOO
CUDDILY	CUDDILY
CASAROL	CASSEROLE
CARABOO	CARIBOU
CITEME2	CITE ME TOO
CUMITED	COMMITTED
CUMQUAT	CUMQUAT
CYTCING	SIGHTSEEING
CYURNO1	SEE WHY YOUR #1
CENERY	SCENERY
CORDELN	CITY IN IDAHO
CONFESS	CONFESS
CNFS2IT	CONFESS TO IT
CHOOZIE	CHOOSIE

CCUREME	SECURE ME
CCUREIT	SECURE IT
CQURIT	SECURE IT
SCUREME	SECURE ME
CHMNYSW	CHIMNEY SWEEP
CFOODS	SEAFOODS
CFOODZ	SEAFOODS
CAWLME1	CALL ME ONE
COLDSWT	COLD SWEAT
CELLDUM	SELDOM
CUZWECU	CAUSE WE SEE YOU
COWSAKI	KAWASAKI MOTORCYCLE
CWASAKI	KAWASAKI MOTORCYCLE
CUZUDUL	CAUSE YOU DULL
CTZMEOW	CATS MEOW
CHPSTIX	CHOPSTICKS
CIFITIZ	SEE IF IT IS
CIFITIS	SEE IF IT IS
CUZIM41	CAUSE I'M FOR ONE
CUZIAM2	CAUSE I'M FOR TOO
CUZIAM1	CAUSE I AM ONE
CYURKUL	SEE WHY YOUR COOL
CALQLUS	CALCULUS
CKRDFLG	CHECKERED FLAG
CITFREE	SEE IT FREE
CHEPSKT	CHEAP SKATE
CQTUOUT	CHECKED YOU OUT
CMYN4SZ	SEE MINE FOR SIZE

"D"

DOIDOIT	DO I DO IT
DRILLME	DRILL ME
DTDOIT2	DON'T DO IT TOO
DSKYZME	DISGUISE ME
DAZNBRD	DAYS NUMBERED
DAZLMYN	DAZZLE MINE
DOITNOW	DO IT NOW
DRILLIT	DRILL IT
DEFALLT	DEFAULT
DFALTD	DEFAULTED
DEFALTD	DEFAULTED
DNTSTOP	DON'T STOP
DNUTSTP	DONUT STOP
DONUTST	DONUT STOP
DEERDO	DEERDO
DEERDUE	DEER DO
DEER1	DEER ONE

DEERONE	DEER ONE
DADSROK	DADS ARE OK
DADZROK	DADS ARE OK
DIZBROD	DIZZY BROAD
DIVRZDO	DIVERS DO
DOGSCAN	DOGS CAN
DOGZCAN	DOGS CAN
DONTCIT	DON'T SEE IT
DEADDUK	DEAD DUCK
DEDDUCK	DEAD DUCK
DEDDUK	DEAD DUCK
DEDUCKT	DEDUCT
DOMEIN	DO ME IN
DOUSIN	DO US IN
DUEUSIN	DO US IN
DUEMEIN	DO ME IN
DONUTSR	DONUTS ARE
DONUTZR	DONUTS ARE
DENYIT	DENY IT
DNYIT	DENY IT
DOITRYT	DO IT RIGHT
DNYIT2	DENY IT TOO
DIDITIN	DID IT IN
DUITSUM	DO IT SOME
DANC4ME	DANCE FOR ME
DOIT2ME	DO IT TO ME
DUITMOR	DO IT MORE
DEPIGME	DEPIGME

DPICTIT	DEPICT IT
DAZLME	DAZZLE ME
DUZFALN	DEWS FALLEN
DRYMEUP	DRY ME UP
DEPIGGD	DEPIGGED
DYITRYT	DIET RIGHT
DYETRED	DYE IT RED
DYETBLUE	DYE IT BLUE
DYETGRA	DYE IT GRAY
DIETDYT	DIET DIET
DUITDEP	DO IT DEEP
DUITDP	DO IT DEEP
DOITFAST	DO IT FAST
DUETFST	DO IT FAST
DADZAKG	DADS A KING
DRTYDOZ	DIRTY DOZEN
DIRTY12	DIRTY DOZEN
DIDUKNO	DID YOU KNOW
DIDUNO	DID YOU KNOW
DPZNDVZ	DIPS N DIVES
DWBHAPY	DON'T WORRY BE HAPPY
DTWBHPY	DON'T WORRY BE HAPPY
DZZDZIT	DIZZY DOES IT
DZYDZIT	DIZZY DOES IT
DED4EVR	DEAD FOREVER
DZITFIT	DOES IT FIT
DIGAHOL	DIG A HOLE
DUBLMYN	DOUBLE MINE

DUDZR4U	DUDS ARE FOR YOU
DIGYURZ	DIG YOURS
DRZROK	DOCTORS ARE OK
DOCZRIN	DOCS ARE IN
DOCSRIN	DOCS ARE IN
DSTROYD	DESTROYED
DUMPEME	DUMPE ME
DUMPME2	DUMPE ME TOO
DUMPIN	DUMPIN
DUMPLIN	DUMPLIN
DUZHENO	DOES HE KNOW
DUZITNO	DOES IT KNOW
DETURZ	DETOURS
DTURZ	DETOURS
DTOHER	DETOURS
DGMYTRK	DIG MY TRUCK
DBAYTME	DEBATE ME
DRYITUP	DRY IT UP
DRIUP	DRY UP
DZETOTZ	DOES EAT OATS
DYNXPNK	DINKS PINK
DTBABUT	DON'T BE A BUTT
DTHZREL	DEATH'S REAL
DTHZPMT	DEATH'S PERMANENT
DATZ4ME	THAT'S FOR ME
DYE4IT2	DYE FOR IT TOO
DIE4IT2	DIE FOR IT TOO
DEFYDME	DIFIED ME

DELAYME	DELAY ME
DLAYZDU	DELAYS DO
DLAYZME	DELAYS ME
DRTYTRX	DIRTY TRICKS
DUZYURZ	DOES YOURS
DAYZND	DAYS END
DAYZEND	DAYS END
DOERAME	DOE RAY ME
DALYDBL	DAILY DOUBLE
DARLING	DARLING
DAIZYMA	DAISY MAE
DRGNFLY	DRAGONFLY
DOBENYC	DO BE NICE
DRIZZLE	LIGHT RAIN
DNGALNG	DINGALING
DTSWTIT	DON'T SWEAT IT
DIPPER	DIPPER
DPTYDU	DIPPETY DO
DPTYDUE	DIPPETY DO
DOGYLVR	DOGGIE LOVER
DUKZBAC	DUCKS BACK
DUKSBAK	DUCKS BACK
DNTFRET	DON'T FRET
DTFGTIT	DON'T FORGET IT
DTKNKIT	DON'T KNOCK IT
DPTYDOG	DEPUTY DOG
DDCTIT	DEDUCT IT
DDKTIT	DEDUCT IT

VANITY PLATE EXPRESSIONS

DUZEKAR	DOES HE CARE
DOGZPOT	DOG SPOT
DMANDIT	DEMAND IT
DEDLOCK	DEADLOCK
DSQLFYD	DISQUALIFIED
DZYNDFY	DIZZY N DAFFY
DIET4ME	DIET FOR ME
DUMPLIN	DUMPLIN
DAPPER	DAPPER
DRAGGIN	DRAGGING
DRAGIN	DRAGGING
DOMINOZ	DOMINOES
DOGWOOD	DOGWOOD
DONGKEY	DONKEY
DAFODIL	DAFFODIL
DFYDUCK	DAFFY DUCK
DRTCHEP	DIRT CHEAP
DRTHARY	DIRTY HARRY
DRTDOZN	DIRTY DOZEN
DOLIKET	DO LIKE IT
DOLIKIT	DO LIKE IT
DTNOKIT	DON'T KNOCK IT
DERILCT	DERELICT
DBLYRMY	DOUBLE YOUR MONEY
DBLUMNY	DOUBLE YOUR MONEY
DRUMRBY	DRUMMER BOY
DANDLYN	DANDELION
DORNOBS	DOOR KNOBS

DORNOBZ	DOOR KNOBS
DUMBTQT	DUMB BUT CUTE
DTBFULD	DON'T BE FOOLED
DTHVALY	DEATH VALLEY
DTBUGME	DON'T BUG ME
DABYDAY	DAY BY DAY
DAYBYDA	DAY BY DAY
DEDMEET	DEAD MEAT
DTBFULZ	DON'T BE FOOLS
DTBSTPD	DON'T BE STUPID
DKSMATE	DUCKS MATE
DKZMAYT	DUCKS MATE
DUEBDUE	DOOBIE DOO
DOBEDO	DOOBIE DOO
DOGSLIF	DOGS LIFE
DOGZLIF	DOGS LIFE
DOGSLYF	DOGS LIFE
DOGZLYF	DOGS LIFE
DADADOC	DAD A DOCTOR
DRAGNET	DRAGNET
DETIGRS	DETROIT TIGERS
DETIGRZ	DETROIT TIGERS
DOLFINS	MIAMI DOLPHINS
DOLSROK	DOLLS ARE OK
DOLZROK	DOLLS ARE OK
DORAYME	DOE RAY ME
DOREME	DO RA ME
DIDDLEE	DIDDLEE

VANITY PLATE EXPRESSIONS

DIDDLE	DIDDLE
DIDDLER	DIDDLER
DRFNATS	STANFORD U BACKWARDS
DELAYME	DELAY ME
DELAYME2	DELAY ME TOO
DOCZUND	DACHSUND DOG
DESTROY	DESTROY
DSTROYR	DESTROYER
DISASTR	DISASTER
DOUNOME	DO YOU KNOW ME
DOIT4ME	DO IT FOR ME
DOIT2ME	DO IT TO ME
DEPDUDU	DEEEP DUDU
DUKTAYL	DUCKTAIL
DUKTAIL	DUCKTAIL
DARNNIX	DARN NICKS
DOCTOR8	DOCTORATE DEGREE
DOCTURT	DOCTORATE DEGREE
DOCKTOR	DOCTOR
DOC	DOCTOR
DRIFIXU	DOCTOR I FIX YOU
DRETTE	DOCTORATE DEGREE
DPCDIVR	DEEP SEA DIVER
DIPTINS	DIPPED IN S***
DIPTNSH	DIPPED IN S***
DRPTBAL	DROPPED BALL
DANGIT	DANG IT
DADRADT	DADRADT (SLANG)

DRTYBDS	DIRTY DIRDS
DRTYBDZ	DIRTY DIRDS
DDYZGRL	DADDYS GIRL
DDYSGRL	DADDYS GIRL
DOBDUE	DO BE DUE
DOOBDOO	DO BE DUE
DOUN2U	DO UNTO YOU
DOUN2YU	DO UNTO YOU
DOUN2ME	DO UNTO ME
DASHFTR	DAY SHIFTER
DIDUNO1	DID YOU KNOW ONE
DOWTIT	DOUBT IT
DBLTRBL	DOUBLE TROUBLE
DVLBEME	DEVIL BE ME
DVLBME	DEVIL BE ME
DREAMER	DREAMER
DUDROPS	DEW DROPS
DUCTIT	DUCT IT
DUCKTIT	DUCKED IT
DUCTAPE	DUCT TAPE
DADSEZE	DADS EASY
DO2OFU	DO TWO OF YOU
DOUWSKI	DO YOU WATERSKI
DEDRALV	DEAD OR ALIVE

"E"

ELECTIT	ELECT IT
ENJOYME	ENJOY ME
EVEDID2	EVE DID TOO
ELEGUNT	ELEGANT
ELEFUNT	ELEPHANT
EZONIN	EAZE ON IN
EASONIN	EASE ON IT
EZONINN	EASE ON IT
ERATIK	ERRATIC
ENUF41	ENOUGH FOR ONE
EZONIN2	EASE ON IN TOO
EGLZFLY	EAGLES FLY
EGLZNST	EAGLES NEST
EQLYZER	EQUALIZER
EQLYZR	EQUALIZER
EZDUZIT	EASY DOES IT
EZMONEY	EASY MONEY

EZEMONY	EASY MONEY
EMTMIND	EMPTY MIND
EVDROPR	EAVENDROPPER
EAGLEZR	EAGLES ARE
EYEDOC	EYE DOCTOR
EYEDOCTR	EYE DOCTOR
ETZHERO	ETS HERO
ETZDUDY	ETS DUDDY
ERLY2RZ	EARLY TO RISE
ERONBOY	ERRAND BOY
EGRBEVR	EAGER BEAVER
EYELUVR	I LOVE HER
ERTHQAK	EARTHQUAKE
FBNEZER	EBENEZER
EQASHUN	EQUATION
ENERGY	ENERGY
ENOUMUS	ENORMOUS
EMBEZLR	EMBEZZLER
ETITALL	EAT IT ALL
EATITAL	EAT IT ALL
EVRGREN	EVERGREEN
EZEXIT	EASY EXIT
EZRYDR	EASY RIDER
EZRYDER	EASY RIDER
EZRYDR	EASY RIDER
EZETYM	EASY TIME
EWER4ME	YOU'R FOR ME
EVRGRST	EVERGREEN STATE

EVRGLDZ	EVERGLADES
EZEXLAX	EASY EXLAX
EZBUCKS	EASY BUCKS
ELAYTED	ELATED
ENYMENY	EANY MEANY
EWERANG	YOU RANG
EMTNEST	EMPTY NEST
ENUFSED	ENOUGH SAID
EZ4U2C	EASY FOR YOU TO SEE
ELDDIP	PIDDLE BACKWARDS
ENUFSEN	ENOUGH SEEN
EXPRESO	COFFEE

"F"

FLIPTIN	FLIPPED IN
FLIPT	FLIPPED
FLOSSIT	FLOSS IT
FLOSSME	FLOSS ME
FIGHTME	FIGHT ME
FREE2ME	FREE TO ME
FREEME2	FREE ME TOO
FITITON	FIT IT ON
FOXRFOX	FOX ARE FOX
FUDBAG	FOOD BAG
FOXYKAT	FOXY CAT
FOXYKTY	FOXY KITTY
FOXYGAL	FOXY GAL
FOXYFOX	FOXY FOX
FOXEEE	FOXY
FLY4ME	FLY FOR ME
FLY4ME2	FLY FOR ME TOO

FIREIT	FIRE IT
FYRITUP	FIRE IT UP
FIREME	FIRE ME
FYRME	FIRE ME
FYRME2	FIRE ME TOO
FYRFLY	FIREFLY
FYRFLYZ	FIRE FLIES
FRFRYS	FRENCH FRIES
FRFRYZ	FRENCH FRIES
FOOTDOC	FOOT DOCTOR
FOOTDR	FOOT DOCTOR
FTDOCTR	FOOT DOCTOR
FLY2ME	FLY TO ME
FEDUP2	FED UP TOO
FUNYGY	FUNNY GUY
FUNYGUY	FUNNY GUY
FUNEGUY	FUNNY GUY
FUNEGAL	FUNNY GAL
FLIPOUT	FLIP OUT
FLUSHED	FLUSHED
FULLBAG	FULL BAG
FRCFRYZ	FRENCH FRIES
FATYNUP	FATTEN UP
FATNUP	FATTEN UP
FLAYKZR	FLAKES ARE
FLAYKSR	FLAKES ARE
FARSYTD	FARSIGHTED
FAKMOUT	FAKEM OUT

FNYBLNY	PHONEY BALONEY
FNYFARM	FUNNY FARM
FOXTROT	FOXTROT
FOXWALK	FOX WALK
FOXWOKS	FOX WALKS
FOXWOKZ	FOX WALKS
FMULAYT	FORMULATE
FYNQLTY	FINE QUALITY
FOGDIN	FOGGED IN
FOGDOUT	FOGGED OUT
FASTEST	FASTEST
FASTAST	FASTEST
FANTAC	FANTASY
FANTSTK	FANTASTIC
FANTACE	FANTASY
FYRZHOT	FIRES HOT
FYRSHOT	FIRES HOT
FREE2U	FREE TO YOU
FREE2U2	FREE TO YOU TOO
FLIPPUR	FLIP HER
FLIPPER	FLIPPER
FREBE2U	FREEBE TO YOU
FORCPTZ	FORCEPTS
FORCPTS	FORCEPTS
FORCEME	FORCE ME
FLY4FRE	FLY FOR FREE
FIZLD	FIZZLED
FIZLDIN	FIZZLED IN

FRAYMME	FRAME ME
FLXIBUL	FLEXIBLE
FYXMYN	FIX MINE
FYXMYN2	FIX MINE TOO
FLORDME	FLOORED ME
FRTFLY	FRUIT FLIES
FRUTFLY	FRUIT FLY
FULMUNE	FULL MOON
FALCUNZ	FALCONS
FALCONZ	FALCONS
FOOD4TH	FOOD FOR THOUGHT
FD4THOT	FOOD FOR THOUGHT
FLANUTS	FULL A NUTS
FULANTZ	FULL A NUTS
FITZOK2	FITS OK TOO
FLIPFLP	FLIPFLOP
FURENZE	FRENZIE
FUN4ALL	FUN FOR ALL
F4GETIT	FORGET IT
FRIKACE	FRICASSEE
FRICASE	FRICASSEE
FRICAC	FRICASSEE
FRACSHN	FRACTION
FRUITLP	FRUIT LOOP
FRUTLUP	FRUIT LOOP
FROOT	FRUIT
FLWRGRL	FLOWER GIRL
FERBALZ	FURBALLS

FURBALZ	FURBALLS
FURBALS	FURBALLS
FERBALS	FURBALLS
FERBALZ	FURBALLS
FULZLVR	FOOLS LOVER
FULANRG	FULL A ENERGY
FULACRP	FULL A CRAP
FRE4U2C	FREE FOR YOU TO SEE
FREE2GO	FREE TO GO
FRKLYNO	FRANKLY NO
FAKTOUT	FAKED OUT
FATCITY	FAT CITY
FEARLUS	FEARLESS
FIGRSKT	FIGURE SKATE
FIREXTR	FIRE EXTINGUISHER
FLYTYE	FLYTIE
FLYTYER	FLYTIER
FISHFRI	FISHFRY
FLYTYEN	FLYTYING
FREXAMZ	FREE EXAMS
F8ZRFUN	FIGURE EIGHTS ARE FUN
FIG8NUT	FIGURE 8 NUT
FIG8DVR	FIGURE 8 DRIVER
FLOOZY	DISREPUTABLE WOMAN
FLOOZIE	DISREPUTABLE WOMAN
FLOOSY	DISREPUTABLE WOMAN
FLOOSIE	DISREPUTABLE WOMAN
FLOPT	FLOPPED

FLOUNTD	FLOUNTED
FANFARE	FANFARE
FANFAYR	FANFARE
FTLDYSG	FAT LADY SINGS
FTLYSGZ	FAT LADY SINGS
FYREATR	FIRE EATER
FYRWOOD	FIREWOOD
FURWOOD	FIR TREE
FLYDOPE	FLYROD DOPE
FLYROD	FLYROD
FLYRODS	FLYRODS
FLYRODZ	FLYRODS
FRAXONS	FRACTIONS
FRAXONZ	FRACTIONS
FORTUNE	FORTUNE
FORHAND	TENNIS TERM
FURTLIS	FERTILIZE
FURTLIZ	FERTILIZE
FLOATER	FLOATER
FLOWTUR	FLOATER
FLOWTER	FLOATER
FEENIZ	PHOENIX, AZ
FASTBUX	FAST BUCK
FIOUTAW	FISH OUTA WATER
FISHRMN	FISHERMAN
FOGCUTR	FOGCUTTER
FUNCEKR	FUNSEEKER
FLYBYNT	FLY BY NIGHT

FLYBNYT	FLY BY NIGHT
FLKMBIC	FLICK MY BIC
FUNSUCR	FUN SUCKER
FZYBEAR	FUZZY BEAR
FZYBEAR	FUZZY BEAR
FISCLED	PHYSICAL EDUCATION
FABRIC8	FABRICATE
FRTLIZR	FERTILIZER
FIZICKS	PHYSICS
FTLOVER	FULL TIME LOVER
FANFT	FANCY FEET
FANCYFT	FANCY FEET
FETLPOZ	FETAL POSITION

"G"

GUFTOFF	GOOFED OFF
GRNGPNS	GROWING PAINS
GRNGPNZ	GROWING PAINS
GRGPANZ	GROWING PAINS
GOLDBRK	GOLD BRICK
GLDBRKR	GOLD BRICKER
GAMZRXG	GAMS ARE EXCITING
GALAXY	GALAXY
GALEXC	GALAXY
GALEXSE	GALAXY
GALAXE	GALAXY
GETGOIN	GET GOIN
GOLFRZR	GOLFERS ARE
GO4GOLD	GO FOR GOLD
GRTIFHD	GREAT IF HARD
GMLOGMD	GIVE ME LIBERYT OR GIVE ME DEATH

GTOFFMB	GET OFF MY BACK
GTOFFIT	GET OFF IT
GOOD2ME	GOOD TO ME
GOOFOFF	GOOF OFF
GOEFAST	GO FAST
GOFASTR	GO FASTER
GOFASTUR	GO FASTER
GITHIGH	GIT HIGH
GIVEINN	GIVE IN
GOFORIT	GO FOR IT
GOFERIT	GO FOR IT
GOPHERT	GO FOR IT
GO4IT	GO FOR IT
GO4IT2	GO FOR IT TOO
GTOFFME	GET OFF ME
GETOFF	GET OFF
GETONIT	GET ON IT
GTCORKT	GET CORKED
GTCROKT	GET CROCKED
GONEWHR	GO ANYWHERE
GDYRZR	GOOD YEARS ARE
GDYRSR2	GOOD YEARS ARE TOO
GIMMEIT	GIMMEIT
GNFISHN	GONE FISHIN
GAMZOVR	GAMES OVER
GIVMEIT	GIVE ME IT
GIVEUP	GIVE UP
GYMPLAZ	JIM PLAYS

GYMZIN	JIM'S IN
GYNZOUT	JIM'S OUT
GYMZADL	JIM'S A DOLL
GYMZGEM	JIM'S GEM
GYNZWET	JIM'S WET
GYMSWET	JIM'S SWEAT
GOODJOB	GOOD JOB
GONCRAZ	GONE CRAZY
GIVITUP	GIVE IT UP
GBY4NOW	GOODBYE FOR NOW
GONNUTS	GONE NUTS
GONNUTZ	GONE NUTS
GIMEMYN	GIMME MINE
GETOFF1	GET OFF ONE
GET1OFF	GET ONE OFF
GNYMGN	GO NORTH YOUNG MAN GO NORTH
GYMTYME	GYM TIME
GREAT2B	GREAT TO BE
GRAZGRA	GRAYS GRAY
GRABIT	GRABIT
GOUP4IT	GO UP FOR IT
GRNZGRN	GREENS GREEN
GRABIT2	GRAB IT TOO
GODN4IT	GO DOWN FOR IT
GIMEABR	GIVE ME A BREAK
GIGL4ME	GIGGLE FOR ME
GENZRIN	JEANS ARE IN

GENZROK	JEANS ARE OK
GIMEABK	GIME A BREAK
GIGL4US	GIGGLE FOR US
GONORTH	GO NORTH
GIGGLES	GIGGLES
GIGGLEZ	GIGGLES
GODZMYN	GOD'S MINE
GETMEUP	GET ME UP
GIGZROK	GIGS ARE OK
GOT2BE	GOT TO BE
GOT2BE1	GOT TO BE ONE
GOT2B1	GOT TO BE ONE
GR2BGR	GREAT TO BE GREAT
GR2BGRT	GREAT TO BE GREAT
GYMEURS	GIMME YOURS
GYMEURZ	GIMME YOURS
GOTALOT	GOT A LOT
GRYNDIT	GRIND IT
GRNDHOG	GROUNDHOG
GAVALOT	GAVE A LOT
GASMEUP	GAS ME UP
GINIPIG	GUINEA PIG
GRASRTS	GRASS ROOTS
GRASRTZ	GRASS ROOTS
GIMEYRZ	GIMME YOURS
GASEMUP	GAS'EM UP
GOPHER1	GO FOR ONE
GUNNUTZ	GUN NUTS

GOFERLV	GO FER LOVE
GOFRLOV	GO FER LOVE
GONNUTZ	GONE NUTS
GUDMRNG	GOOD MORNING
GONFSHN	GONE FISHING
GON2CIT	GONE TO SEE IT
GIMEABR	GIME A BREAK
GLDSLPR	GOLD SLIPPER
GONHNTN	GONE HUNTIN
GOOUT2C	GO OUT TO SEE
GREMLIN	GREMLIN
GIMEHI5	GIMME HIGH 5
GYMEHI5	GIMME HIGH 5
GON2SEA	GONE TO SEA
GOBLINZ	GOBLINS
GRNDAX	GRIND AXE
GDOLBOY	GOOD OL BOY
BLDBRKN	GOLD BRICKIN
GYGL4WE	GIGGLE FOR WE
GDHUMUR	GOOD HUMOR
GRSHOPR	GRASSHOPPER
GRASHPR	GRASSHOPPER
GDHUMR	GOOD HUMMER
GTUPNGO	GET UP AN GO
GONEPLC	GO ANY PLACE
GDLVZSC	GOOD LOVER SCARCE
GYNIPIG	GUINEA PIG
GRAYZME	GRAZE ME

GO4ITIF	GO FOR IT IF
GOODFUN	GOOD FUN
GON2HVN	GONE TO HEAVEN
GEODUCK	GEODUCK
GUZBERY	GOOSEBERRY
GUSBERY	GOOSEBERRY
GLBTRTR	GLOBETROTTER
GLSBOTM	GLASS BOTTOM
GR82B12	BREAT TO BE ONE TOO
GR8BODY	GREAT BODY
GTSMART	GET SMART
GOLFSYN	GOLF SYNDROME
GOEFUR	GOPHER
GOGGLES	GOGGLES
GOOGLES	GOOGLES
GOLRUSH	GOLD RUSH
GARDNER	GARDENER
GEEWHIZ	GEE WHIZ
GWHIZ	GEE WHIZ
GIDLUV2	GEE I'D LOVE TOO
GILUVU	GEE I LOVE YOU
GILUV2	GEE I LOVE YOU TOO
GILUVYU	GEE I LOVE YOU
GNGRSNP	GINGER SNAP
GURUNDR	GEE YOU ARE UBDRESSED
GURQT	GEE YOU ARE CUTE
GUROK	GEE YOU ARE OK
GUROK2	GEE YOU ARE OK TOO

GYMEABK	GIMME A BREAK
GRAVDGR	GRAVE DIGGER
GODUTCH	GO DUTCH
GASHOG	GASHOG
GASBRNR	GAS BURNER
GLFSYNR	GOLF SINNER/SWEARS
GINRUMY	GIN RUMMY
GLASBLR	GLASS BLOWER
GLASCTR	GLASS CUTTER
GLFCLBZ	GOLF CLUBS
GLDNGAT	GOLDEN GATE
GDAKSHN	GOOD ACTION
GOODLSR	GOOD LOSER
GOODLZR	GOOD LOSER
GUNSMOK	GUNSMOKE
GALAMYN	GAL A MINE
GRINGO	GRINGO
GUDEVNG	GOOD EVENIG
GOODACT	GOOD ACT
GUTLESS	GUTLESS
GRUNTS2	GRUNTS TOO
GRUNTZ2	GRUNTS TOO
GLDFISH	GOLD FISH
GOLDFSH	GOLD FISH
GLDNAGE	GOLDEN AGE
GTOBLST	GHETTO BLASTER
GTOBTR	GHETTO BLASTER
GTOBLSR	GHETTO BLASTER

GO4ADNK	GO FOR A DUNK
GITANET	GET A NET
GETANET	GET A NET
GRUNTER	GRUNTER
GETLIT	GET LIT
GTLITUP	GET LIT UP
GET2IT	GET TO IT
GETTOIT	GET TO IT
GODWNDP	GO DOWN DEEP
GUTBSTR	GUT BUSTER
GETAJOB	GET A JOB
GO4IT4U	GO FOR IT FOR YOU
GRSHFTR	GRAVE SHIFT
GNTLBEN	GENTLE BEN
GETALYF	GET A LIFE
GO2PCS	GO TO PIECES
GO2POT	GO TO POT
GETAKEN	GET TAKEN
GTBELTD	GET BELTED
GONEAPE	GONE APE
GON2POT	GONE TO POT
GIVME12	GIVE ME ONE TOO
GUDJUNK	GOOD JUNK
GITITIN	GET IT IN
GETITIN	GET IT IN

"H"

H8WORK	HATE WORK
HIGHUP	HIGHUP
H2OMELN	WATERMELON
HAPYGAL	HAPPY GAL
H20ZFYN	WATERS FINE
HAYTNIT	HATE N IT
H204ME	WATER FOR ME
H204US	WATER FOR US
HORIZN	HORIZON
H20SKIR	WATERSKIER
HOTCAKS	HOT CAKES
HOTCAKZ	HOT CAKES
HOTROD	HOTROD
HOTRODR	HOTRODDER
HIBUNKY	HI BUNKY
HOTNHVY	HOT N HEAVY
HYRYZEN	HIGH RISIN

HYRYSN	HIGH RISIN
HOLDIGR	HOLEDIGGER
HALINAS	HAULIN A**
HEYGALZ	HEY GALS
HEYGALS	HEY GALS
HOTZY	HOTSY
HOTSY	HOTSY
HOP2HUR	HOPE TO HER
HOWIZIT	HOW IS IT
HOWISIT	HOW IS IT
HOTZTZY	HOTSY-TOTSY
HOTZYSY	HOTSY-TOTSY
H82BEYU	HATE TO BE YOU
H82BEU	HATE TO BE YOU
H82CUGO	HATE TO SEE YOU GO
HOTWATR	HOT WATER
HOTH20	HOT WATER
HOTZNYC	HOTS NICE
HOWZMYN	HOWS MINE
HINSITE	HINDSITE
HYNSYTE	HINDSITE
HOTBUTR	HOT BUTTER
HOWZYRZ	HOWS YOURS
HOWKENW	HOW CAN YOU
HAZTOBE	HAS TO BE
HAZ2BEE	HAS TO BE
HAZ2BE	HAS TO BE
HAZ2B	HAS TO BE

HAZTUBE	HAS TO BE
HAZTOB	HAS TO BE
H8GIRLS	HATE GIRLS
H8GIRLZ	HATE GIRLS
HATEDRS	HATE DOCTORS
HOPTOUR	HOP TO HER
HOWCANU	HOW CAN YOU
HORSEDO	HORSE DOO
HOP4ME2	HOPE FOR ME TOO
HIFLYER	HIGH FLYER
HIFLIER	HIGH FLYER
HARD2C	HARD TO SEE
HARD2B	HARD TO BE
HARZ2YU	HERES TO YOU
HARZTOU	HERES TO YOU
HOPSRIN	HOPS ARE IN
HOPZRIN	HOPS ARE IN
HIZIZIT	HIS IS IT
HAIRS2U	HAIRS TO YOU
HAIRZ2U	HAIRS TO YOU
HARD2CU	HARD TO SEE YOU
HATZOFF	HATS OFF
HATSOFF	HATS OFF
HOTFOX	HOT FOX
HIGHDOC	HIGH DOC
HIGHDOK	HIGH DOCK
HOTNRG	HOT ENERGY
HOTENRG	HOT ENERGY

HANNAH	SAME FW & BW
HNKYDRE	HUNKY DORIE
HOTPOTZ	HOT POTS
HARDRIF	HARDER IF
HOTBOX	HOT BOX
HOTBOXZ	HOT BOXES
HUMPTDT	HUMPTY DUMPTY
HUMTDMT	HUMPTY DUMPTY
HPYGLFR	HAPPY GOLFER
HANGON	HANG ON
HARD4ME	HARD FOR ME
HIGLOSS	HIGH GLOSS
HOTBUNS	HOT BUNS
HOTBUNZ	HOT BUNS
HTCRBNS	HOT CROSS BUNS
HTCRBNZ	HOT CROSS BUNS
HOGWILD	HOG WILD
HARZ14U	HERES ON FOR YOU
HE2LYS	HE TOO LAYS
HE2LYZ	HE TOO LAYS
HICLASS	HIGH CLASS
HRTNMYN	HURTIN MINE
HAPEGUY	HAPPY GUY
HARD2DO	HARD TO DO
HISHUZ	HIGH SHOES
HIPOCTS	HIGH POCKETS
HIPOCTZ	HIGH POCKETS
HRTMYN2	HURT MINE TOO

HAPYGAL	HAPPY GAL
HORSLVR	HORSE LOVER
HORZLVR	HORSE LOVER
HARMUNY	HARMONY
HAWYAN	HAWAIIAN
HELPME	HELP ME
HILPME2	HELP ME TOO
HANDME1	HAND ME ONE
HARTAKZ	HEARTACHES
HAMHOCS	HAM HOCKS
HAMHOCZ	HAM HOCKS
HDOVRHL	HEAD OVER HEELS
HARTAYK	HEARTACHE
HEDZRUP	HEADS ARE UP
HWHIZUP	HOW HIGHS UP
HYIZFYN	HIGH IS FINE
HARDNOX	HARD KNOCKS
HARRYGY	HAIRY GUY
HAIRYGY	HAIRY GUY
HLYMCRL	HOLY MACKEREL
HARDNXZ	HARD KNOCKS
HDNOXZ	HARD KNOCKS
HGITUP	HANG IT UP
HNGITUP	HANG IT UP
HOTFYRS	HOT FIRES
HOTFYRZ	HOT FIRES
HEATZON	HEATS ON
HAFCOCT	HALF COCKED

HAFCOKT	HALF COCKED
HOTNUZ	HOT NEWS
HARTLES	HEARTLESS
HWDUUDU	HOW DO YOU DO
HWDOUDO	HOW DO YOU DO
HETOLYZ	HE TOO LIES
HE2LIES	HE TOO LIES
HYNZYNY	HINES TINY
HOTSHTZ	HOT SHORTS
HAF2GO2	HAVE TO GO TO
HALFWIT	HALFWIT
HIJNXME	HIGH JINX ME
HCKYFAN	HOCKEY FAN
HIONLST	HIGH ON LIST
HIIQZR1	HIGH IQ'S ARE #1
HVYDUDY	HEAVY DUTY
HEDOHLZ	HEAD OVER HELLS
HAVABAL	HAVE A BALL
HVAHPDA	HAVE A HAPPY DAY
HSEWRKR	HOUSE WRECKER
HMEWRKR	HOME WRECKER
HOTWHLZ	HOT WHEELS
HIPDEEP	HIP DEEP
HOZENOZ	HOSE NOSE
HIHIPZ	HIGH HIPS
HOTIRON	HOT IRON
HOZNOZR	HOSE NOSER
HUNYZDU	HONIES DO
HENOSIT	HE KNOWS IT

HOWDEE	HOWDIE
HARDROC	HARD ROCK
HARDROK	HARD ROCK
HARDROX	HARD ROCK
HOLFAST	HOLD FAST
HOOKTUP	HOOKED UP
HUMGBRD	HUMMING BIRD
HEVENLY	HEAVENLY
HARDER2	HARDER TOO
HRTGRTY	HERTY GERTY
HRDAZHL	HARD AS H***
HOLYCOW	HOLY COW
HOLECOW	HOLY COW
HEDSTRG	HEAD STRONG
HYDNSEK	HIDE N SEEK
HYDNCEK	HIDE N SEEK
HCKYNUT	HOCKEY NUT
HERKANZ	HURRICANES
HAFMOON	HALF MOON
HALIBUT	HALIBUT
HRYPITZ	HARRY PITZ
HDRUSTR	HEAD ROOSTER
HLYLZDS	HOLY LIZARDS
HLYLZDZ	HOLY LIZARDS
HEARWER	HERE WE WERE
HEREWER	HERE WE WERE
HAVACOW	HAVE A COW
HADAV8	HADA V8
HADACOW	HAD A COW

HOGCALR	HOG CALLER
HELPME2	HELP HE TOO
HRTFLGS	HURT FEELINGS
HRTFLGZ	HURT FEELINGS
HRTMEGD	HURT ME GOOD
HEREME2	HEAR ME TOO
HEARME2	HEAR ME TOO
HITOPS	HIGH TOPS
HITOPZ	HIGH TOPS
HISHUZ	HIGH SHOES
HUGHSTN	HOUSTON, TEXAS
HYDNSEK	HIDE N SEEK
HINAYBR	HIGH NEIGHBOR
HIJUMPR	HIGH JUMPER
HRSHUZE	HORSESHOES
HORSHUZ	HORSESHOES
HOOTOWL	HOOTOWL
HOWL4ME	HOWL FOR ME
HUM4ME	HUM FOR ME
HOOTZ2	HOOTS TOO
HOOTS3	HOOTS TOO
HOWLS2	HOWLS TOO
HOWLZ2	HOWLS TOO
HUMMS2	HUMMS TOO
HUMMZ2	HUMMS TOO
HTDGBUN	HOTDOG BUN
HYUDUDE	HIGH YOU DUDE
HCKLBRY	HUCKLBERRY
HENHOUS	HEN HOUSE

HENHOWS	HEN HOUSE
HENYPNY	HENNY PENNY
HNYPENY	HENNY PENNY
HLICPTR	HELICOPTER
HRGLASS	HOUR GLASS
HEYTAXI	HEY TAXI
HOTNKY	HOT N CRANKY
HOTPOKR	HOT POKER
HUGMINE	HUG MINE
HYABUBY	HI A BUBY
HIBUNKY	HI BUNKY
HIGHDOC	HI DOC
HIGHDOCK	HIGH DOCK
HOTBUX	HOT BUCKS
HOOTERS	HOOTERS
HOOTERZ	HOOTERS
HEYUGAL	HEY YOU GAL
HAYUGAL	HEY YOU GAL
HAF2FIT	HAVE TO FIT
HUMDRUM	HUMDRUM
HOEHUM	HO HUM
HUREUP	HURRY UP
HWYHONY	HIGHWAY HONEY
HWYHUNY	HIGHWAY HONEY
HRS2GO	OURS TO GO
HRZ2BRN	HOURS TO BURN
HYJACT	HIJACKED
HYJAKT	HIJACKED
HEYJUDE	HEY JUDE

HAF1000	HALF GROSS
HOSTYLE	HOSTILE
HAPY14U	HAPPY ONE FOR YOU
HOOME	WHO ME
H2OPYPE	WATERPIPE
H20PIPE	WATERPIPE
H2OMILL	WATER MILL
H2OWEEL	WATER WHEEL
H2ODROP	WATER DROP
H2OMIZR	WATER MIZER
H2OBAG	WATER BAG
H2OPADL	WATER PADDLE
HDNOCKR	HEAD KNOCKER
HOLEHOG	WHOLE HOG
HONKIFU	HONK IF YOU
HOBNOBR	LOODE TONGUE
HELP4U	HELP FOR YOU
HLYSMOK	HOLY SMOKE
HYADOLL	HI YA DOLL
HYATRKY	HI YA TURKEY
HYABABE	HI YA BABE
HOTNJCY	HOT AN JUICY
H2OFALZ	WATER FALLS
H2OFALLS	WATER FALLS
H2OGUNS	WATER GUNS
H2OGUNZ	WATER GUNS
H2OGUN	WATER GUN

"I"

ITZAL4U	IT'S ALL FOR YOU
ILYKIT	I LIKE IT
ILIKIT2	I LIKE IT TOO
IMKLENE	I'M CLEAN
IBARFT	I BARFED
IBARFT2	I BARFED TOO
ITSELLS	IT SELLS
IDBARF2	I'D BARF TOO
IFUCAN	IF YOU CAN
IFITZYU	IF IT'S YOU
IFUCAN2	IF YOU CAN TOO
ITSFREE	IT'S FREE
ITZFREE	IT'S FREE
IZLUVOK	IS LOVE OK
ITCEBUT	ITCE BUTT
ICUROK	I SEE YOU ARE OK
IBLUIT	I BLEW IT

IBLUEIT	I BLEW IT
ITZMYTM	IS MY TIME
IDIGYOU	I DIG YOU
IFITSOK	IF IT'S OK
IFITZOK	IF IT'S OK
ITZNEW2	IT'S NEW TOO
IFITZ	IF IT IS
IDIGU	I DIG YOU
IDIGU2	I DIG YOU TOO
ISLECU	I'LL SEE YOU
ISLECU2	I'LL SEE YOU TOO
ITZNEWZ	IT'S NEWS
IZITTRU	IS IT TRUE
IZITRUE	IS IT TRUE
ITSHARD	IT'S HARD
ITZHARD	IT'S HARD
INORDER	IN ORDER
ITZBAD	IT'S BAD
IM2SICK	I'M TOO SICK
ITSTUFF	IT'S TOUGH
ITZTUFF	IT'S TOUGH
ICITSOK	I SEE IT'S OK
ICITZOK	I SEE IT'S OK
ITZGOOD	IT'S GOOD
IFITZME	IF IT'S ME
IFITSME	IF IT'S ME
IFURGOD	IF YOU ARE GOOD
IFUGOOD	IF YOU ARE GOOD

ITSOK2	IT'S OK TOO
IFUHONK	IF YOU HONK
ITSPITZ	IT'S THE PITS
ITZPITZ	IT' THE PITS
I2R4YU	I TOO ARE FOR YOU
IZR4ME	EYES ARE FOR ME
IMYRLDR	I'M YOUR LEADER
IDOC	EYE DOC
IDOCTOR	EYE DOCTOR
IMAGONR	I'M A GONER
IMGREAT	I'M GREAT
IFITSU2	IF IT'S YOU TOO
IMGONE	I'M GONE
INNOUT	IN N OUT
ITZLUST	IT'S LUST
ITSHUNG	IT'S HUNG
IFITZYU	IF IT'S YOU
IMGONE2	I'M GONE TOO
IM4SALE	I'M FOR SALE
IM4SAYL	I'M FOR SALE
INJOYIT	ENJOY IT
ITZHUNG	IT'S HUNG
IDUIT4U	I DO IT FOR YOU
ILSHOYU	I'LL SHOW YOU
ITSCOOL	IT'S COOL
ITZCOOL	IT'S COOL
ITHOTSO	I THOUGHT SO
ISHUTR2	I SHUTTER TOO

ISHUTR	I SHUTTER
IDNYIT	I DENY IT
IMFEDUP	I'M FED UP
ITSWIMS	IT SWIMS
ITSWIMZ	IT SWIMS
ILY24U	I LIE TO FOR YOU
ILY24YU	I LIE TO FOR YOU
ILY4U	I LIE FOR YOU
ILY4YU	I LIE FOR YOU
ILY4YOU	I LIE FOR YOU
ILUV2GO	I LOVE TO GO
ITSALL1	IT'S ALL ONE
ITSNOTK	IT'S NO TRICK
IZKENIN	IS KEN IN
ITZALL1	IT'S ALL ONE
INCUMIN	INCOMING
IFITZNC	IF IT'S NICE
ICUR2	I SEE YOU ARE TOO
IZITTRU	IS IT TRUE
ICURQT	I SEE YOU ARE CUTE
ILAY4U2	I LAY FOR YOU TOO
IZMYBIZ	IS MY BUSINESS
IQUITIT	I QUIT IT
ICUR4ME	I SEE YOU ARE FOR ME
ICANCU	I CAN SEE YOU
ITISTRU	IT IS TRUE
ITBRZME	IT BORES ME
IRUNIT	I RUN IT

IRONIT	IRON IT
IHATEU	I HATE YOU
ITZTRUE	IT'S TRUE
ITZALIN	IT'S ALL IN
IHAYTIT	I HATE IT
IHAYTU	I HATE YOU
IMLAYZ2	I'M LAZY TOO
ITSAL4U	IT'S ALL FOR YOU
ISMYEXN	IS MY EX IN
ITELLU	I TELL YOU
ITRYDIT	I TRIED IT
ITZTIME	IT'S TIME
ITSTIME	IT'S TIME
IMDULL	I'M DULL
ITFIGRZ	IT FIGURES
ITWORKZ	IT WORKS
ITRVLLT	I TRAVEL LIGT
ITVLTOO	I TRAVEL TOO
IMYOURS	I'M YOURS
IMYORZ	I'M YOURS
ITSCORN	IT'S CORN
ITZCORN	IT'S CORN
ITZCRNY	IT'S CORNY
ITZTYM2	IT'S TIME TOO
I2R4U	I TOO ARE FOR YOU
ITS4ME	IT'S FOR ME
IDIGIT	I DIG IT
ITFITZ	IT FITS

IMYOUZ2	I'M YOURS TOO
ISYRZOK	IS YOURS OK
IZMYTYM	IS MY TIME
IMSTEWD	I'M STEWED
ILIKEIT	I LIKE IT
ITZMYBG	IT'S MY BAG
ITZMBAG	IT'S MY BAG
IZ4U2	EYES FOR YOU TOO
IZR4U	EYES ARE FOR YOU
IZR4U2	EYES ARE FOR YOU TOO
ITWOCAN	I TOO CAN
IORDRD1	ORDERED ONE
IZ2BBLU	IS TO BE BLUE
IZ2BLU	IS TOO BLUE
IZ2BLUE	IS TOO BLUE
ISBORD2	IS BORED TOO
IBORDIT	I BORED IT
INHIDET	IN HIGH DEBT
IAM2PLZ	I AIM TO PLEASE
ITFLOFF	IT FELL OFF
ITZNAUT	IT'S NAUGHTY
ITZ24TM	IT'S TWO FOUR TIME
ISHUDA	I SHOULDA
ITANTSO	IT AIN'T SO
ITZ4TYM	IT'S FOR TIME
IFYURGD	IF YOUR GOOD
IROK2U	I ARE OK TO YOU
IDOITAL	I DO IT ALL

IDUITAL	I DO IT ALL
ITDPNDZ	IT DEPENDS
IROCKU2	I ROCK YOU TOO
INSTLUV	ISTANT LOVE
ITZ2QET	IT'S TOO QUIET
ILVJRKS	I LOVE JERKS
ILVJRKZ	I LOVE JERKS
ITZINIT	IT'S IN IT
ITFIGRZ	IT FIGURES
IMLIVID	I'M LIVID
IMFREZN	I'M FREEZIN
IZ2ATEE	IS TO A TEE
IMLIVIN	I'M LIVIN
INMYIZ	IN MY EYES
INMY2IZ	IN MY TWO EYES
IZLVBLD	IS LOVE BLIND
IBOXTIT	I BOXED IT
ICURMAD	I SEE YOU ARE MAD
ITZLAYT	IT'S LATE
ESYTZOK	EYESIGHTS OK
INMYDMZ	IN MY DREAMS
INYRDMZ	IN YOUR DREAMS
IM2ROOD	I'M TOO RUDE
IM2RUDE	I'M TOO RUDE
INDIGOE	INDIGO
ISYTZGD	IYESIGHTS GOOD
INDUTYM	IN DUE TIME
ITZLEGL	IT'S LEGAL

IGUANA	IGUANA
ICYKNOT	I SEE WHY NOT
ITZABIZ	IT'S A BUSINESS
IFLYIT2	I FLY IT TOO
INAKLIK	IN A CLIQUE
INAKLIC	IN A CLIQUE
INRELFM	IN REAL FORM
INRARFM	IN RARE FORM
IBNYC2U	I BE NICE TO YOU
INIT4U	IN IT FOR YOU
INIT4ME	IN IT FOR ME
INIT4YU	IN IT FOR YOU
ITZPITZ	IT'S PITS
IMACPA	I'M A CPA
ILYALOT	I LIE A LOT
ICUCAN2	I SEE YOU CAN TO
IMAWINR	I'M A WINNER
INDRVST	IN DRIVERS SEAT
IMRELVD	I'M RELIEVED
ILBYURZ	I'LL BUY YOURS
ITFIZLD	IT FIZZLED
IFSHUFZ	IF SHOE FITS
ILTRY2	I'LL TRY TO
ISLETRY	I'LL TRY
ITBURNS	IT BURNS
ITBURNZ	IT BURNS
ITSMELS	IT SMELLS
ITSMELZ	IT SMELLS

IFITZ4U	IF IT'S FOR YOU
ITFITZ	IT FITS
ITFYTZ	IT FITS
IMHYPER	I'M HYPER
ITZUP2U	IT'S UP TO YOU
IZRONU	EYES ARE ON YOU
IDYD4IT	I DIED FOR IT
ITZUP4U	IT'S UP FOR YOU
ITDZFYT	IT DOES FIT
IRONMAN	IRONMAN
IFUCIT	IF YOU SEE IT
ISEW4YU	I SEW FOR YOU
ITZMBAG	IT'S MY BAG
INFVROF	IN FAVOR OF
IFWECIT	IF WE SEE IT
ILSHOYU	I'LL SHOW YOU
IFYURSR	IF YOURS ARE
IFYURZR	IF YOURS ARE
ITLCSTU	IT'LL COST YOU
INDAZWK	IN A DAYS WORK
INSULTN	INSULTIN
ITCBITC	ITSY BITSY
ITZNEW2	IT'S NEW TOO
ITSTNKZ	IT STINKS
INSLTME	INSULT ME
INJOYU2	IN ENJOY YOU TO
ITIZ4U	IT IS FOR YOU
INJOYIT	IN ENJOY IT

ITELUTR	I TELL YOU TRUTH
IDSPYZU	I DESPISE YOU
IMPDQ2	I'M PRETTY DAMN QUICK TO
IBLUSH	I BLUSH
ILEAGLE	SICK BIRD
INAKOMA	IN A COMA
I41WILL	I FOR ONE WILL
IC2FEET	I SEE TWO FEET
ISPYD4U	I SPIED FOR YOU
IWOOD2	I WOULD TO
ITLHURT	IT'LL HURT
INS4CAR	INSURANCE FOR CAR
INKZDRY	INKS DRY
INKSDRY	INKS DRY
ITDUZIT	IT DOES IT
ITWURKZ	IT WORKS
IFURGIT	I FORGET
IFUR12	IF YOU ARE ONE TOO
IFUR1TO	IF YOU ARE ONE TOO
ICUDB12	I COULD BE ONE TOO
IFYRFRE	IF YOU'RE FREE
ICYRAHD	I SEE YOU'RE AHEAD
IMPROVZ	IMPROVISE
IMAFL4U	I'M A FOOL FOR YOU
IDOBE12	I DO BE ONE TOO
IWOKLBR	I WORK LOVER
IMTORQT	I'M TORQUED
ICQUOUT	I SEEK YOU OUT

IMTUKRD	I'M TUCKERED
IZITITE	IS IT TIGHT
ISITITE	IS IT TIGHT
ITSPDUP	IT'S PAID UP
ITZPDUP	IT'S PAID UP
ITZPD4	IT'S PAID FOR
ITINMAN	ITINMAN
INVADRS	INVADERS
INVADRZ	INVADERS
ICQTU2	I SEEKED YOU TOO
IDROPS	EYE DROPS
IDROPZ	EYE DROPS
ICECULR	ICE COOLER
ICECLER	ICE COOLER
ICECLR	ICE COOLER
ISOLATE	ISOLATE
ITSF8	IT'S FATE
IMACLTS	I'M A CLUTS
IMACLTZ	I'M A CLUTS
ILCKU41	I'LL CHECK YOU FOR ONE
INOHOW2	I KNOW HOW TO
ICOUDLVU	I COULD LOVE YOU
IMBKRPT	I'M BANKRUPT
IMBROKE	I'M BROKE
IMLODED	I'M LOADED
IMLOST	I'M LOST
IMLOST2	I'M LOST TOO
IMCNFSD	I'M CONFUSED

IMCNFZD	I'M CONFUSED
IMYURZ	I'M YOURS
IMYOUS	I'M YOURS
IMYOURS	I'M YOURS
IMYOURZ	I'M YOURS
IMONLY1	I'M ONLY ONE
IMTIRED	I'M TIRED
IMTYRED	I'M TIRED
ITSUXIF	IT SUCKS IF
IFITSUX	IF IT SUCKS
IDIOTIC	IDIOTIC
IFELTRZ	I FELL TREES
IFLTREZ	I FELL TREES
ILOGGER	I LOGGER
ILOGIT	I LOG IT
IDAGO4U	IDA GO FOR YOU
IVAMIND	I'VE A MIND
IVAMND2	I'VE A MIND TO
INXDRY	INKS DRY
IZRONYU	EYES ARE ON YOU
ITSUX	IT SUCKS
ICURXTD	I SEE YOU ARE EXCITED
ILVBOYS	I LOVE BOYS
ILVBOYZ	I LOVE BOYS
ILBDIPT	I'LL BE DIPPED
IZOK4U	EYES OK FOR YOU
IZOK4YU	EYES OK FOR YOU
IM4URLV	I'M FOR YOUR LOVE

INAMNUT	IN A MINUTE
IDRICYU	EYE DOCTOR I SEE YOU
IDRICU	EYE DOCTOR I SEE YOU
IRFZTWO	I REFUSE TOO
IREFZTOO	I REFUSE TOO
IREFUZ2	I REFUSE TOO
IBTFARM	I BOUGHT FARM
IBOTFRM	I BOUGHT FARM
IOUXTLO	I OWE YOU EXACTLY O
IOUXLEO	I OWE YOU EXACTLY O
ISNOALL	IS KNOW ALL
IZNOALL	IS KNOW ALL
IMISTIT	I MISSED IT
INOITIS	I KNOW IT IS
ISITTRU	IS IT TRUE
ICKYIKY	REAL BAD
ITHAS2B	IT HAS TO BE
IFNOT4U	IF NOT FOR YOU
IBNICE2	I BE NICE TOO

"J"

JOG4ME2	JOG FOR ME TOO
JOG4ME	JOG FOR ME TOO
JOGMEIN	JOG ME IN
JOG4ME	JOG FOR ME
JIS4JOY	"J" IS FOR JOY
JOXRJOX	JOCKS ARE JOCKS
JOY2NO	JOY TO KNOW
JOY2NOU	JOY TO KNOW YOU
JOY2ME	JOY TO ME
JOY2ME2	JOY TO ME TOO
JOY2U	JOY TO YOU
JOY2ALL	JOY TO ALL
JURYRING	JURYRIG
JRYRIGD	JURY RIGGED
JELYROL	JELLY ROLL
JELEROL	JELLY ROLL
JUST4ME	JUST FOR ME

JUST4WE	JUST FOR WE
JKWUZQK	JACK WAS QUICK
JRKZONU	JERKS ON YOU
JRKSRIN	JERKS ARE IN
JOCZONU	JOKES ON YOU
JENIFUR	JENNIFER
JOISTME	JOIST ME
JAMBME	JAMBME
JUPITER	JUPITER
JUSAMIN	JUST A MINUTE
JSTAMIN	JUST A MINUTE
JOENOZE	JOE KNOWS
JOKZONU	JOKES ON YOU
JLEBELE	JELLY BELLY
JUMP2IT	JUMP TO IT
JUMPIN	JUMPING
JUBLE	JUBILEE
JACNJIL	JACK AND JILL
JACNJYL	JACK AND JILL
JKBQUIK	JACK BE QUICK
JLYFISH	JELLY FISH
JSTTHNK	JUST THINK
JTTHYNK	JUST THINK
JUS4FUN	JUST FOR FUN
JSTDOZN	JUST DOZZING
JUS4U2C	JUST FOR YOU TO SEE
JUMPNBN	JUMPING BEAN
JMPNBEN	JUMPING BEAN
JUGLMYN	JUGGLE MINE

JIGLMYN	JIGGLE MINE
JACOLTN	JACK-O-LATERN
JAMNJEL	JAM AND JELLY
JUGGLED	JUGGLER
JUGLRVN	JUGULAR VEIN
JUSTBU	JUST BE YOU
JUSTBEU	JUST BE YOU
JUSTBYU	JUST BE YOU
JUSTBME	JUST BE ME
JALOPEZ	JALOPIES
JAILBRD	JAIL BIRD
JSTATOY	JUST A TOY
JUNKHEP	JUNK HEAP
JUS4FUN	JUST FOR FUN
JUS4LOV	JUST FOR LOVE
JUMPJAC	JUMP JACK
JUMPJAK	JUMP JACK
JUSBUMN	JUST BUMMIN
JSTBUMN	JUST BUMMIN
JAWBOWN	JAW BONE
JUSTASK	JUST ASK
JKBQUIK	JACK BE QUICK
JSTGRUP	JUST GROW UP
JUMPEM	JUMP'EM
JURAFEE	GIRAFFE
JABRBOX	JABBER BOX
JUSTASK	JUST ASK
JUST4U	JUST FOR YOU
JUSTHPY	JUST HAPPY

"K"

KEPQUYT	KEEP QUIET
KTZMEOW	CAT MEOW
KALICO	CALICO
KINGKNG	KING KONG
KNGKONG	KING KONG
KTZWSKR	CATS WHISKERS
KOOLIT	COOL IT
KRANOPR	CRANE OPERATOR
KUZUCME	CAUSE YOU SEE ME
K9IZADG	K9 IS A DOG
K9ZADOG	K9 IS A DOG
KENISIN	KEN IS IN
KENIZIN	KEN IS IN
K9SADOG	K9'S A DOG
KPQYET	KEEP QUIET
KNGSTBL	KINGS TABLE
K9LUVR	K9 LOVER

K9LOVER	K9 LOVER
KEPQYET	KEEP QUIET
KAKAZBS	KAKAS BULLSHIT
KYDZDO	KIDS DO
KIDSDUE	KIDS DO
KEYPQYT	KEEP QUIET
KSNCZNS	KISS N COUSINS
KSNCSNZ	KISS N COUSINS
KARUTZ	CARROTS
KAROTS	CARROTS
KYDZCAN	KIDS CAN
KUTYPIE	CUTIE PIE
KUTIEPY	CUTIE PIE
KIDZRIT	KIDS ARE IT
KIDZLUV	KIDS LOVE
KPASCRT	KEEP A SECRET
KISSMYN	KISS MINE
KISMINE	KISS MINE
KPIT4ME	KEEP IT FOR ME
KISMYN2	KISS MINE TOO
KGKOBRA	KING COBRA
KGCOBRA	KING COBRA
K8ISFYN	KATE IS FINE
K8IZFYN	KATE IS FINE
KNYNKYD	CANINE KID
KATZRQT	CATS ARE CUTE
KRKAKRP	CROCK A CRAP
KNOTS2U	NUTS TO YOU

KNOT4U	NOT FOR YOU
KNOT4US	NOT FOR US
KAYAKIT	KAYAK IT
KAYAK	KAYAK
KIKNBUT	KICKIN BUT
KIKBUNZ	KICK BUNS
KISMYFT	KISS MY FOOT
KISMY12	KISS MY FOOT
KLONDYK	KLONDIKE
KANGURU	KANGAROO
KELARGO	KEY LARGO
KNOTURT	NOT YOUR TURN
KYTFLYR	KITE FLIER
KENUBME	CAN YOU BE ME
KNKYKID	KINKY KID
KOPYKAT	COPY CAT
KNKYGUY	KINKY GUY
KULDOWN	COOL DOWN
KAYAKER	KAYAKER
KISADTH	KISS A DEATH
KNOGUTS	NO GUTS
KNOWGTS	NO GUTS
KNOGUTZ	NO GUTS
KYOTE	COYOTE
KNOTSEW	NOT SO
KNOTTY1	NAUGHTY ONE
KNOTONU	NOT ON YOU
KNOT4U	NOT FOR YOU

KNOT2B	NOT TO BE
KAYAKNG	KAYAKING
KLUNKER	OLD CAR
KEYPQYT	KEEP QUIET
KEEPQYT	KEEP QUIET
KNITPKR	KNIT PICKER
KNITWIT	KNITWIT
KNOTME2	NOT ME TOO
KNOT4ME	NOT FOR ME

"L"

LVSNUZN	LOVE SNOZZIN
LVSNUSN	LOVE SNOZZIN
LAYDNEZ	LAY DOWN EASY
LVZGRAT	LOVE GREAT
LVZGR8T	LOVE GREAT
LVFISHN	LOVE FISHING
LAWZDAZ	LOUSY DAYS
LITLTGR	LITTLE TIGER
LILTIGR	LITTLE TIGER
LILTYGR	LITTLE TIGER
LVRZDU2	LOVERS DO TOO
LVRZDO2	LOVERS DO TOO
LYTMFYR	LIGHT MY FIRE
LVBATHZ	LOVE BATHS
LVBATHS	LOVE BATHS
LVCOYNZ	LOVE COINS
LVBEGLZ	LOVE BEAGLES

LETZMIX	LETS MIX
LBROFLV	LABOR OF LOVE
LVHR4ME	LEAVE HER FOR ME
LVHM4ME	LEAVE HIM FOR ME
LVOREOS	LOVE OREOS
LVOREOZ	LOVE OREOS
LVYRHAR	LOVE YOUR HAIR
LVURIZ	LOVE YOUR EYES
LOTSALV	LOTSA LOVE
LOTZALV	LOTSA LOVE
LIVENUP	LIVEN-UP
LIVINUP	LIVEN-UP
LYONME	LIE ON ME
LYONME2	LIE ON ME TOO
LUVURIZ	LOVE YOUR EYES
LOSTMYN	LOST MINE
LOSTMIN	LOST MIND
LODOWN	LOW DOWN
LOVE2	LOVE TOO
LOVETOO	LOVE TOO
LOVEME	LOVE ME
LOVEME2	LOVE ME TOO
LUVCOPS	LOVE COPS
LUVCOPZ	LOVE COPS
LETMEIN	LET ME IN
LOVEUTO	LOVE YOU TOO
LAYZYAS	LAZY AS
LAMEDWN	LAY ME DOWN

LETITB	LET IT BE
LETITBE	LET IT BE
LUVRBOY	LOVER BOY
LETMEBE	LET ME BE
LUVLIFE	LOVE LIFE
LUVLYFE	LOVE LIFE
LOVENU	LOVEN YOU
LOVENU2	LOVEN YOU TOO
LUVINU2	LOVEN YOU TOO
LYTMEUP	LIGHT ME UP
LIZ4LUV	"L" IS FOR LOVE
LYFISTO	LIFE IS TOO
LIFEIZ2	LIFE IS TOO
LOVEU2	LOVE YOU TOO
LOVEYU2	LOVE YOU TOO
LYFRDTH	LIFE OR DEATH
LIFEGZON	LIFE GOES ON
LYFGZON	LIFE GOES ON
LYFSABC	LIFES A BITCH
LAMDUCK	LAME DUCK
LAYMDUK	LAME DUCK
LUV2TVL	LOVE TO TRAVEL
LUV2TRV	LOVE TO TRAVEL
LAYPRSN	LAY PERSON
LAYPRZN	LAY PERSON
LOVLYAS	LOVELY AS
LAYITON	LAY IT ON
LAITON	LAY IT ON

LALADY	L.A. LADY
LVZGYZ	LOVER GUYS
LVYRBDY	LOVE YOUR BODY
LVME2U	LEAVE ME TO YOU
LVME2YU	LEAVE ME TO YOU
LUVLIPS	LOVE LIPS
LUVLIPZ	LOVE LIPS
LVYRLPS	LOVE YOUR LIPS
LVYRLPZ	LOVE YOUR LIPS
LTSMKUP	LET'S MAKE UP
LTZMKUP	LE'TS MAKE UP
LOCITON	LOCK IT ON
LEGUNT	ELEGANT
LEFUNT	ELEPHANT
LEFUNTS	ELEPHANT
LEFUNTZ	ELEPHANT
LETRRIP	LET HER RIP
LVALWAZ	LOVE ALL WAYS
LKBWITU	LUCK BE WITH YOU
LVZURZ2	LOVES YOURS TOO
LVYRZTO	LOVE YOURS TOO
LVMYNTO	LOVE MINE TOO
LUK4US2	LUCK FOR US TOO
LKB4ULP	LOOK BEFORE YOU LEAP
LVSGRAT	LOVES GREAT
LVZGRAT	LOVES GREAT
LVMYRAT	LOVE MY RAT
LV4EVER	LOVE FOREVER

LUV4EVR	LOVE FOREVER
LVZ4EVR	LOVES FOREVER
LEDME2U	LEAD ME TO YOU
LEDMEON	LEAD ME ON
LUSGUSE	LOOSE GOOSE
LUZGUSE	LOOSE GOOSE
LZRDLVR	LIZARD LOVER
LIZLUZR	"L" IS FOR LOSER
LPNZCIT	LICENSED PRACTICAL NURSES SEE IT
LPNZDO2	LICENSED PRACTICAL NURSES DO TOO
LPNSCAN	LICENSED PRACTICAL NURSES CAN
LPNZCAN	LICENSED PRACTICAL NURSES CAN
LUVMUNY	LOVE MONEY
LVMONEY	LOVE MONEY
LVYURIZ	LOVE YOUR EYES
LUVURIZ	LOVE YOUR EYES
LTZSPLT	LET'S SPLIT
LZ4LAZY	L'S FOR LAZY
LVRLVIT	LOVE OR LEAVE IT
LVMELVR	LEAVE ME LOVER
LFSABCH	LIFES A BEACH
LV4ME2	LOVE FOR ME TOO
LUV4ME2	LOVE FOR ME TOO
LVDBYAL	LOVED BY ALL

LVBYALL	LOVE BY ALL
LV4EYZ	LOVE FOR EYES
LV4EYES	LOVE FOR EYES
LOVE4IZ	LOVE FOR EYES
LUV4EYZ	LOVE FOR EYES
LKALYK	LOOK ALIKE
LUKALYK	LOOK ALIKE
LKALYKS	LOOK ALIKE
LKALYKZ	LOOK ALIKE
LOKALYK	LOOK ALIKE
LKME4ME	LIKE ME FOR ME
LETUSBE	LET US BE
LETUS B	LET US BE
LETUZB	LET US BE
LETUSBE	LET US BE
LNGJONS	LONG JOHNS
LNGJONZ	LONG JOHNS
LYD4ME2	LIED FOR ME TOO
LY4ME	LIED FOR ME
LIE4ME	LIE FOR ME
LIE4ME2	LIE FOR ME TOO
LVMYDOC	LOVE MY DOCTOR
LYNCHME	LYNCH ME
LVRZLKU	LOVERS LIKE YOU
LYGLIZD	LEGALIZED
LEGLIZD	LEGALIZED
LIZRDZR	LIZARDS ARE
LIZRDZ	LIZARDS

LVMYLIZ	LOVE MY LIZ
LETUSC2	LETTUCE SEE TOO
LETTUSB	LETTUCE BE
LETUSB2	LETTUCE BE TOO
LVJKRZ2	LOVE JOKERS TOO
LOTZALV	LOTS OF LOVE
LOTSALV	LOTS OF LOVE
LAPDOGZ	LAP DOGS
LDYFNGER	LADYFINGER
LASAGNA	LASAGNA
LILWAIF	LITTLE WIFE
LVSGLLF	LOVE SINGLE LIFE
LVSINLF	LOVE SINGLE LIFE
LVJUGS	LOVE JUGS
LVJUGZ	LOVE JUGS
LILTYKE	LITTLE TYKE
LTLTYKE	LITTLE TYKE
LVNTEKS	LOVE ANTIQUES
LVNTEKZ	LOVE ANTIQUES
LILBUGR	LITTLE BUGGER
LTSMKDL	LETS MAKE DEAL
LTZMKDL	LETS MAKE DEAL
LUGNUTS	LUGNUTS
LUGNUTZ	LUGNUTS
LOTZARM	LOTS A ROOM
LOTSARM	LOTS A ROOM
LVB4UGO	LOVE BEFORE YOU GO
LVPARTZ	LOVE PARTIES

LVPRTEZ	LOVE PARTIES
LTRYWNR	LOTTERY WINNER
LOTRYWR	LOTTERY WINNER
LVMETNR	LOVE ME TENDER
LVMETDR	LOVE ME TENDER
LVCATLE	LOVE SEATTLE
LOBSTER	LOBSTER
LOYERS	LAWYERS
LOYERZ	LAWYERS
LISN2ME	LISTEN TO ME
LV2TCH	LOVE TO TEACH
LV2TECH	LOVE TO TEACH
LV2TCHU	LOVE TO TEACH YOU
LVSHOPG	LOVE SHOPPING
LVSHPNG	LOVE SHOPPING
LECTRCN	ILECTRICIAN
LOCKTUP	LOCKED UP
LAFTER	LAUGHTER
LAFTUR	LAUGHTER
LITNING	LIGHTNING
LYTNING	LIGHTNING
LVAFOOL	LOVE A FOOL
LVGRKFD	LOVE GREEK FOOD
LUVTCBY	LOVE TCBY
LOSYLVR	LOUSY LOVER
LZYLOVR	LOUSY LOVER
LILSQRT	LITTLE SQUIRT
LUVBLTZ	LOVE BAC, LET, TOM

LIFZADG	LIFES A DRAG
LIFZADR	LIFES A DRAG
LVCRCDZ	LOVE CREDIT CARDS
LVTTRLG	LOVE TRAVEL TRAILERING
LGSPLTR	LOG SPLITTER
LEGLADE	LEGAL AIDE
LEGLAID	LEGAL AIDE
LOBSTRZ	LOBSTERS
LOBSTUR	LOBSTERS
LOBSTER	LOBSTERS
LVWKNDZ	LOVE WEEKENDS
LVWKNDS	LOVE WEEKENDS
LVVEGEZ	LOVE VEGETABLES
LVPITZA	LOVE PIZZA
LVPETZA	LOVE PIZZA
LEPRCON	LEPRICON
LVURMDR	LOVE YOUR MOTHER
LVYRMDR	LOVE YOUR MOTHER
LVURFDR	LOVE YOUR FATHER
LVYRFDR	LOVE YOUR FATHER
LVURKDZ	LOVE YOUR KIDS
LVYRKDZ	LOVE YOUR KIDS
LVURSIS	LOVE YOUR SISTER
LVYRSIS	LOVE YOUR SISTER
LUNCHBX	LUNCH BOX
LNCHBOX	LUNCH BOX
LADYLUK	LADY LUCK
LDYLUCK	LADY LUCK

LOVEETC	LOVE AND SOFORTH
LVXTCEE	LOVE ECSTASY
LOVRBOY	LOVER BOY
LSYDEAL	LOUSY DEAL
LZYDEAL	LOUSY DEAL
LASTCAL	LAST CALL
LSTCALL	LAST CALL
LITLHLP	LITTLE HELP
LITLONE	LITTLE ONE
LVQTPIZ	LOVE CUTIE PIE
LARAMS	LOS ANGELES RAMS
LARAMZ	LOS ANGELES RAMS
LALAKRS	LOS ANGELES LAKERS
LALAKRZ	LOS ANGELES LAKERS
LEPFROG	LEAP FROG
LAZBONE	LAZY BONE
LMNADE	LEMONADE
LEMNADE	LEMONADE
LMNAID	LEMONADE
LFTWGTS	LIFT WEIGHTS
LUXURY	LUXURY
LAFALOT	LAUGH A LOT
LOWRPM	LOW RPM
LUSMUSE	LOOSE MOOSE
LVMYKTY	LOVE MY KITTY
LVUSO41	LOVE YOU SO FOR ONE
LETITAL	LET IT ALL
LITLFAT	LITTLE FAT

LVORBST	LOVE OR BUST
LVOVLYF	LOVE OF LIFE
LVMYWYF	LOVE MY WIFE
LVYA2DT	LOVE YOU TO DEATH
LTZDICR	LET'S DICKER
LTZDIKR	LET'S DICKER
LVABUPY	LOVE A PUPPY
LITENUP	LIGHTEN UP
LYTENUP	LIGHTEN UP
LY1OUUP	LIGHTEN YOU UP
LIVENUP	LIVEN UP
LVAPRTR	LOVE A PARTNER
LVADOPE	LEAVE A DOPE
LVSEX2I	LEAVE SEX TO I
LYTLOAD	LIGHT LOAD
LORYDR	LOW RIDER
LOWRYDR	LOW RIDER
LPGLZDS	LEAPING LIZARDS
LPGLZDZ	LEAPING LIZARDS
LV2RASL	LOVE TO WRESTLE
LVMISRY	LOVE MISERY
LVMIZRY	LOVE MISERY
LVMIZRE	LOVE MISERY
LVMISRE	LOVE MISERY
LVME4ME	LOVE ME FOR ME
LVME4LF	LOVE ME FOR LIFE
LVBUTEE	LOVE BEAUTY
LEGSRIN	LEGS ARE IN

LEGZRIN	LEGS ARE IN
LEGSRUP	LEGS ARE UP
LEGZRUP	LEGS ARE UP
LVME10R	LOVE ME TENDER
LOLIPOP	LOLIPOP
LOTSNRV	LOTS OF NERVE
LOTANRV	LOTS OF NERVE
LILWIMP	LITTLE WIMP
LILBITR	LITTLE BITTER
LV2FISH	LOVE TO FISH
LV2JOG	LOVE TO JOG
LVJOGIN	LOVE JOGGING
LOVE2CU	LOVE TO SEE YOU
LILMOUS	LITTLE MOUSE
LTLMOUS	LITTLE MOUSE
LZYLUVR	LAZY LOVER
LAIDBAC	LAID BACK
LAIDBAK	LAID BACK
LVIT2ME	LEAVE IT TO ME
LAYDBAK	LAID BACK
LOPROFL	LOW PROFILE

"M"

MESSY1	MESSY ONE
MYNZFRZ	MINE'S FROZE
MKMEHPY	MAKE ME HAPPY
MULTRAN	MULE TRAIN
MITRBOX	MITRE BOX
MSEHOUS	MOUSE HOUSE
MNSTRKR	MOON STREAKER
METCUTR	MEAT CUTTER
MYXTUP	MIXED UP
MYXTUP2	MIXED UP TOO
MYNZ4GD	MINES FOR GOOD
MYNZ4SL	MINES FOR SALE
MNZ4SAL	MINES FOR SALE
MYNZFRE	MINES FREE
MNZFREE	MINES FREE
MTGPMTS	MORTGAGE PAYMENTS
MTGPMTZ	MORTGAGE PAYMENTS

MYBONZR	MY BONES ARE
MYBONES	MY BONES
MYBIZIZ	MY BUSINESS IS
MYBIZIS	MY BUSINESS IS
MILNAIR	MILLIONAIRE
MILNAYR	MILLIONAIRE
MILBRBY	MILLION DOLLAR BABY
MILDLBB	MILLION DOLLAR BABY
MILDUDE	MILDUDED
MYLDUE	MILDUE
MYLDUED	MILDUED
MYLDUDE	MILDUED
MYNSBRK	MINE'S BROKE
MYNZBRK	MINE'S BROKE
MSPIGGY	MISS PIGGY
MSTEWED	AM STEWED
MSTEWD2	AM STEWED TOO
MOOVOVR	MOVE OVER
MUVOVR	MOVE OVER
MUVOVER	MOVE OVER
MYTFYN	MIGHTY FINE
MYTEFYN	MIGHTY FINE
MYTFINE	MIGHTY FINE
MISTUTO	MISSED YOU TOO
MISTUT2	MISSED YOU TOO
MYNISOK	MINE IS OK
MYNIZOK	MINE IS OK
MEDDOC	MEDICAL DOCTOR

MDCLDOC	MEDICAL DOCTOR
ME4U	ME FOR YOU
ME4YU	ME FOR YOU
ME4YOU	ME FOR YOU
ME4YU2	ME FOR YOU TOO
ME4YOU2	ME FOR YOU TOO
MASTITE	MA'S TIGHT
MAZTITE	MA'S TIGHT
MYNZOLD	MINE'S OLD
MANOZIT	MA KNOWS IT
MYTURN	MY TURN
MAKMYDA	MAKE MY DAY
MUSTBME	MUST BE ME
MEUPTO	ME UP TOO
MEUPTOU	ME UP TO YOU
MEUP2	ME UP TOO
MYJOBIS	MY JOB IS
MYJOBIZ	MY JOB IS
MUMS4ME	MOM'S FOR ME
MUMZME	MOM'S FOR ME
MABOYET	MA BE QUIET
MYNZWET	MINE'S WET
MYNZDRY	MIN'S DRY
MAKITDO	MAKE IT DO
MAKITDU	MAKE IT DO
MYTRYK	MY TRIKE
MYTRUCK	MY TRUCK
MYTRICK	MY TRICK

MYNSTYT	MINE'S TIGHT
MYNZTYT	MINE'S TIGHT
MYNSRDY	MINE'S READY
MYNZRDY	MINE'S READY
MYSCHEF	MISCHIEF
MISCHEF	MISCHIEF
MYNSDED	MINE'S DEAD
MYNZDED	MINE'S DEAD
MYNZDRY	MINE'S DRY
MYNZDRI	MINE'S DRY
MY69ZOK	MY 69'S OK
MYAS	MY A**
MAZWEL	MAY AS WELL
MAYZWEL	MAY AS WELL
MINUSYU	MINUS YOU
MINUSU	MINUS YOU
MYNUSU	MINUS YOU
MYNUSYU	MINUS YOU
MYNWKS	MINE WORKS
MYNWRKS	MINE WORKS
MYNWKZ	MINE WORKS
MYNWRKZ	MINE WORKS
MYNSGRA	MINE'S GRAY
MINSGRA	MINE'S GRAY
MTRSICL	MOTORCYLE
MOMSIN	MOM'S IN
MOMZIN	MOM'S IN
MOMSIN2	MOMS IN TOO

MOMZIN2	MOMS IN TOO
MOMSAQN	MOMS A QUEEN
MOMZAQN	MOMS A QUEEN
MARYME	MARRY ME
MEMARY	ME MARY
MARYME2	MARRY ME TOO
MARYUS	MARRY US
ME2MARY	ME TOO MARRY
ME2HOT	ME TOO HOT
ME2SHOT	ME TOO SHOT
MESHUTR	ME SHOOTER
MYSHUZE	MY SHOES
METRU2U	ME TRUE TO YOU
MYNZMYN	MINE'S MINE
MYNGROS	MINE GROSS
MYNGROZ	MINE GROSS
MMMGOOD	MMM GOOD
MYNHRTS	MINE HURTS
MYNHRTZ	MINE HURTS
MUNBAYB	MOON BABY
MYLOVIS	MY LOVE IS
MYLOVIZ	MY LOVE IS
MYASGON	MY A** GONE
MSIKOVU	AM SICK OF YOU
MSIKOFU	AM SICK OF YOU
MYNZFNY	MINE'S FUNNY
MYNSFNY	MINE'S FUNNY
MNZCRZY	MINE'S CRAZY

MYNUBIS	MINE YOUR BUSINESS
MYNUSIZ	MINE YOUR BUSINESS
MISTUSE	MISUSE
MYRNDUS	MY R.N. DOES
MYRNDUZ	MY R.N. DOES
MYNGROZ	MINE GROWS
MYNGROS	MINE GROSS
MMIZRAT	MICKEY MOUSE IS RAT
MAGNJGS	MAGGIE N JIGGS
MAGNGZ	MAGGIE N JIGGS
MYNSPDQ	MINE'S PDQ
MYNZPDQ	MINE'PDQ
MYNROTN	MINE ROTTEN
MYIZ4YU	MY EYES FOR YOU
MYIZR4U	MY EYES ARE FOR YOU
MISTWET	MIST WET
MSTYWET	MISTY WET
MSTUWET	MISSED YOU WET
MYNSQTR	MINE'S CUTIER
MYNZQTR	MINE'S CUTIER
MYSUNSR	MY SONS ARE
MYSUNZR	MY SONS ARE
MYSUNIS	MY SON IS
MYSUNIZ	MY SON IS
MTRSYKO	MOTORCYCLE
MOMWOW	SAME FWD AND BKWD
MELOWME	MELLOW ME
MVOVREZ	MOVE OVER EASY

MLKSHKS	MILKSHAKES
MLKSHKZ	MILKSHAKES
MELODEZ	MELODIES
MELODYZ	MELODIES
MSPIGGB	MISS PIGGY BROTHER
MAKMYNU	MAKE MINE YOU
MEM24U	ME AM TOO FOR YOU
MEM24YU	ME AM TOO FOR YOU
MER24U	ME ARE TOO FOR YOU
MILKMAN	MILKMAN
MKYGRNR	MONKEY GRINDER
MKYGRDR	MONKEY GRINDER
MKEYLOVR	MONKEY LOVER
MYNDYED	MINE DIED
MINEDID	MINE DID
MYDEZIL	MY DIESEL
MYDEZL	MY DIESEL
MYNZFVR	MINE'S FOREVER
MYNKLIK	MINE CLICK
MYNSKPZ	MINE SKIPS
MYNSKPS	MINE SKIPS
MYNMISZ	MINE MISSES
MYNJRKS	MINE JERKS
MYNJRKZ	MINE JERKS
MYNJRK2	MINE JERK TOO
MNZNFYR	MINE'S UNFIRE
MTMINDS	EMPTY MINDS
MTMINDZ	EMPTY MINDS

MOLEHOL	MOLE HOLE
MOLHOLE	MOLE HOLE
MERMAYD	MERMAID
MUSKETO	MOSQUITO
MSNBELS	MISSION BELLS
MSNBELZ	MISSION BELLS
MEDYSYN	MEDICINE
MUKLUKS	MUKLUKS
MUKLUKZ	MUKLUKS
MUSKRAT	MUSK RAT
MSBHAVN	MISBEHAVIN
MISTU2	MISSED YOU TOO
MSTUSEW	MISSED YO SO
MISTUSO	MISSED YOU SO
MAYBSIX	MAYBE SIX
MAYBESX	MAYBE SIX
MY1DSYR	MY ONE DESIRE
MY1DZYR	MY ONE DESIRE
MADREMR	AMA DREAMER
MIRMAYD	MERMAID
MADIETR	AM A DIETER
MUNSHYN	MOONSHINE
MUNLYT	MOON LIT
MOONLYT	MOONLIT
MUNLYTE	MOONLIGHT
MUNELYT	MOONLIT
MAXNUTZ	MACK'S NUTS
MAXNUTS	MACK'S NUTS

MKYSHYN	MONKEYSHINE
MESMRIZ	MESMIRIZE
MEZMRIZ	MESMIRIZE
MMISRAT	MICKEY MOUSE IS RAT
MMZMRAT	MICKEY MOUSE IS MIDGET RAT
MENUROK	MEN YOU ARE OK
MESARND	MESS AROUND
MESNRND	MESSIN ROUN
MULTRAN	MULETRAIN
MUMBLER	MUMBLER
MUMBLES	MUMBLES
MOCASYN	MOCCASIN
MOCASIN	MOCCASIN
MARBULS	MARBLES
MARBULZ	MARBLES
MANSHUN	MANSION
MSTRAP	MOUSETRAP
MSETRAP	MOUSETRAP
MISLTOW	MISTLETOE
MISTLTO	MISTLETOE
MUSTURD	MUSTARD
MAMMUTH	MAMMOTH
MYEQUIL	MY EQUAL
MYEQUAL	MY EQUAL
MYEQULE	MY EQUAL
MYEQUL	MY EQUAL
MYSTIFY	MYSTIFY
MNDBOGL	MIND BOGGLE

M2SHORT	AM TOO SHORT
M2TALL	AM TOO TALL
MOO2UTO	MOO TO YOU TOO
MOO2YU2	MOO TO YOU TOO
MOO2U2	MOO TO YOU TOO
MEDRUPT	ME DOCTOR YOU PATIENT
MAYONAZ	MAYONNAISE
MTLWRKR	METAL WORKER
MEDRRDR	METER READER
MORGAGZ	MORTGAGES
MISSLED	MISLED
MISLEAD	MISLED
MOLASUS	MOLASSES
MIZZURI	MISERY
MAFLWR	SAILING SHIP
MERIMAC	SAILING SHIP
MPROVIZ	IMPROVISE
MBEZLUR	EMBEZZLER
MBRZLR	EMBEZZLER
MAYONAS	MAYONAISSE
MAYBEE	MAYBE
MAYBE4U	MAYBE FOR YOU
MAYBESO	MAYBE SO
MSGIDUD	MISGUIDED
MSGYDED	MISGUIDED
MSBHAVN	MISBEHAVIN
MKRUM4U	MAKE ROOM FOR YOU
MTROTYM	MATTER OF TIME

MTRATYM	MATTER OF TIME
MECQOUT	ME SEEK YOU OUT
MAHOGNY	MAHOGANY
MNCHKIN	MUNCHKIN
MONKEES	MONKEYS
MONKEEZ	MONKEYS
MUNKEYS	MONKEYS
MUNGKEZ	MONKEYS
MUNSTRS	MUNSTERS
MUNSTRZ	MUNSTERS
MILBRWR	MILWAUKEE BREWERS
MINTWIN	MINNESOTA TWINS
MNTWINS	MINNESOTA TWINS
MNTWINZ	MINNESOTA TWINS
MAMAYI	MA MAY I
MAYIMA	MAY I MA
MPLSRP	MAPLE SYRUP
MPLSURP	MAPLE SYRUP
MOOLA	MONEY
MARINER	MARINER
MNTRJAC	MONTEREY JACK
MYWRECK	MY WRECK
MATIGER	MOMMA TIGER
MYLSURG	MY LOSS YOUR GAIN
MTROFFT	MATTER OF FACT
ME2NOU	ME TO KNOW YOU
ME2KNOU	ME TO KNOW YOU
ME2NOYU	ME TO KNOW YOU

MTSTHLN	MT ST HELENS
MUDFLOW	MUD FLOW
MYTAXI	MY TAXI
MYTAXEE	MY TAXI
MELOOUT	MELLOW OUT
MNTNDEW	MOUNTAIN DEW
MTNDEW	MOUNTAIN DEW
MTNDUE	MOUNTAIN DEW
MNTNDUE	MOUNTAIN DEW
MNTNDO	MOUNTAIN DEW
MTNDUE	MOUNTAINDEW
MUSLTUF	MUSCLE TOUGH
MSLTUFF	MUSCLE TOUGH
MJTTIRD	AM JUST TIRED
MMYZBOY	MOMMIES BOY
MYHMZ4U	MY HOMES FOR YOU
MAFTRU2	AM AFTER YOU TOO
MOVNTYM	MOVING TIME
MACANIK	MECHANIC
MUVITON	MOVE IT ON
M4MAN	AM FOREMAN
MOMSEZE	MOMS EASY
MUSSOPO	OPOSSUM BACKWARDS
MOWHAIR	MOHAIR
MOKASIN	MOCCCASIN
M4UONLY	AM FOR YOU ONLY
MALUGOT	AM ALL YOU GOT
MY CHOYC	MY CHOICE

MYCHOYS	MY CHOICE
MYAPT4U	MY APARTMENT FOR YOU
MSLSWRK	MISSILES WORK
MSLZWRK	MISSILES WORK
MEBETOO	ME BET TOO
MEBETOU	ME BET YOU

"N"

NOALMNY	NO ALIMONY
NOMOOLA	NO MONEY
NO12MRY	NO ONE TO MARRY
NSULTIN	INSULTIN
NSULTAN	INSULTIN
NSULTME	INSULT ME
NE14LUV	ANYONE FOR LOVE
NJOYIT	ENJOY IT
NJOYME	ENJOY ME
NJOYUS	ENJOY US
NOTICTS	NO TICKETS
NOTICTZ	NO TICKET
NURSEME	NURSE ME
NOMORE2	NO MORE TO
NOREST	NO REST
NOT2DAY	NOT TODAY
NOFREEB	NO FREEB

NOSENSE	NO SENSE
NOCENTS	NO SENSE
NOCENTZ	NO SENSE
NOSENTZ	NO SENSE
NONOTFIT	NONE OF IT
NUNOFIT	NONE OF IT
NUNOVIT	NONE OF IT
NOT4ME2	NOT FOR ME TOO
NOT4ME	NOT FOR ME
NOTICKE	NO TICKET
NORELEF	NO RELIEF
NOMO4ME	NO MORE FOR ME
NOISIT	NO IS IT
NOIZIT	NO IS IT
NOSWEAT	NO SWEAT
NYTLYFE	NIGHT LIFE
NYTLYF	NIGHT LIFE
NOWUCAN	NOW YOU CAN
NOWUKEN	NOW YOU CAN
NOT2BE	NOT TO BE
NOT2BE	NOT TO BE ME
NOT2B	NOT TO BE
NOT2BE1	NOT TO BE ONE
NYDTYME	NIGHTY TIME
NYDTYME	NIGHTY TIME
NITETYM	NIGHTY TIME
NOWISNO	NOW IS NO
NOWIZNO	NOW IS NO

NDYTME	INDICT ME
NDYTME2	INDICT ME TOO
NOT4NOW	NOT FOR NOW
NOT4NEW	NOT FOR NEW
NERELF	ANY RELIEF
NORELF	NO RELIEF
NORELEF	NO RELIEF
NETYM4U	ANY TIME FOR YOU
NVR2LAT	NEVER TOO LATE
NOITALL	KNOW IT ALL
NEURBIZ	ANY YOUR BUSINESS
NEURBYZ	ANY YOUR BUSINESS
NOTMJOB	NOT MY JOB
NTMYJOB	NOT MY JOB
NOISOUT	NO IS OUT
NOSEOUT	NOSE OUT
NYTZR4U	NIGHTIES ARE FOR YOU
NOIZIT	NO IS IT
NOIZIT2	NO IS IT TOO
NOXQSIS	NO EXCUSES
NOXQSIZ	NO EXCUSES
NOXQSYS	NO EXCUSES
NE14ME	ANYONE FOR ME
NE14ME2	ANYONE FOR ME TOO
NTSOFST	NOT SO FAST
NICE2BE	NICE TO BE
NICE2B	NICE TO BE
NYCTOBE	NICE TO BE

NICE2B1	NICE TO BE ONE
NYC2NOU	NICE TO KNOW YOU
NERSYTD	NEARSIGHTED
NOTFRME	NOT FOR ME
NOTINIT	NOT IN IT
NSYDOUT	INSIDE OUT
NO1WINS	NO ONE WINS
NO1WINZ	NO ONE WINS
NOTYM4U	NO TIME FOR YOU
NITIT4U	KNIT IT FOR YOU
NOMO4ME	NO MORE FOR ME
NOPAYDA	NO PAY DAY
NT2REST	NOT TO REST
NO2REST	NO TO REST
NYDENYT	NIGHTIE NIGHT
NOGOALS	NO GOALS
NOGOALZ	NO GOALS
NOWYNNR	NO WINNER
NOWINER	NO WINNER
NOZITIN	NOSE IT IN
NOPAYNS	NO PAINS
NOPAYNZ	NO PAINS
NORESN2	NO REASON TO
NOSHEET	NO SHEET
NOSHETS	NO SHEETS
NOSHETZ	NO SHEETS
NE1WILD	ANYONE WILD
NE2WILD	ANY TWO WILD

NORST4U	NO REST FOR YOU
NOSUCLK	NO SUCH LUCK
NETAKRS	ANY TAKERS
NETAKRZ	ANY TAKERS
NOTACLU	NOT A CLUE
NOTAKLU	NOT A CLUE
NE1WIL2	ANYONE WILL TOO
NE1WOOD	ANYONE WOULD
NE1WUD2	ANYONE WOULD TOO
NE1SHUD	ANYONE SHOULD
NE14ME	ANYONE FOR ME
NE14ME2	ANYONE FOR ME TOO
NOTMYIZ	NOT MY EYES
NOTMYID	NOT MY IDENTIFICATION
NTFULDK	NOT FULL DECK
NTFLDEK	NOT FULL DECK
NOTLNG2	NOT LONG TO
NOTLONG	NOT LONG
NOTLNG4	NOT LONG FOR
NOYRBIZ	KNOW YOUR BUSINESS
NOSNRDN	NO SOONER DONE
NDURME	ENDURE ME
NDUR4ME	ENKURE FOR ME
NJOYMLV	ENJOY MY LOVE
NO1BTME	NO ONE BUT ME
NOWUCIT	NOW YOU SEE IT
NOWUDNT	NOW YOU DON'T
NE14T42	ANYONE FOR TEA FOR TWO

NE14T	ANYONE FOR TEA
NE14TEA	ANYONE FOR TEA
NE14PRT	ANYONE FOR PARTY
NE14PAT	ANYONE FOR PAT
NYFTY1	NIFTY ONE
NIMFO	NYNPHO
NYTLYT	NIGHT LIGHT
NYTLYTS	NIGHT LIGHT
NYTLYTZ	NIGHT LIGHT
NEPTOON	NEPTUNE
NEP2NE	NEPTUNE
NOCHSPT	NO CHILD SUPPORT
NTRPRIZ	ENTERPRISE
NOWIWON	SAME FW & BW
NOUTURN	NO U TURN
ENERGEE	ENERGY
NRG	ENERGY
NEGEE	ENERGY
NKITOFFF	KNOCK IT OFF
NUGGETS	NUGGETS
NGRAVER	ENGRAVER
NAILDUP	NAILED UP
NGINEER	ENGINEER
NOTR2IT	NO TRICK TO IT
NTURTYP	NOT YOUR TYPE
NTURTRN	NOT YOUR TURN
NOMADIC	A WANDERER
NOFURQS	NO FURTHER QUESTIONS

NOFURQZ	NO FURTHER QUESTIONS
NTZNBTZ	NUTS N BOLTS
NOUDRWY	NO OTHER WAY
NOUDRWA	NO OTHER WAY
NORESN2	NO REASON TO
NOREZN2	NO REASON TO
NTGLEFT	NOTHING LEFT
NO12CME	NO ONE TO SEE ME
NO12CU	NO ONE TO SEE YOU
NO12CYU	NO ONE TO SEE YOU
NO12LOV	NO ONE TO LOVE
NO12FEL	NO ONE TO FEEL
NVRGREN	NEVER GREEN
NETIME	ANYTIME
NETIME2	ANYTIME TO
NOLIPSV	NO LIP SERVICE
NYANKEZ	NEW YOUK YANKEES
NIKATYM	NICK OF TIME
NICATYM	NICK OF TIME
NOPNNOG	NO PAIN NO GAIN
NE4PKR	ANYONE FOR POKER
NE1NETM	ANYONE ANYTIME
NSOMNIA	INSOMNIA
NO2NDS	NO SECONDS
NO2NDZ	NO SECONDS
NORSN2B	NO REASON TO BE
NORZN2B	NO REASON TO BE
NORUM4U	NO ROOM FOR YOU

NETHG4U	ANYTHING FOR YOU
NETHING	ANYTHING
NOBTSAL	NO BUTTS ALLOWED
NOBTZAL	NO BUTTS ALLOWED
NTHEBAG	IN THE BAG
NYNICKS	NEW YORK KNICKS
NOFUFU	NO FUFU
NOFOOFU	NO FUFU
NOFULIN	NO FOOLIN
NORPM	NO RPM
NOGUTS	NO GUTS
NOGUTZ	NO GUTS
NEKLESS	NECKLASS
NEKLUSS	NECKLASS
NE1421	ANYONE FOR 21
NE14ANY	ANYONE FOR ANY
NE14NE1	ANYONE FOR ANYONE
NE14ANE	ANYONE FOR ANNIE
NOTSOB	BOSTON BACKWARDS
NOTSOBD	NOTSO BAD
NEKNUDE	NECK NUDE
NOCIGAR	NO CIGAR
NOSEGAR	NO CIGAR
N10CITY	ENTENCITY
NOIMNOT	NO I'M NOT
NLIOME	ENLIGHTEN ME
NLIGH10	ENLIGHTEN
NLIE10	ENLIGHTEN

NLIE10U	INLIGHTEN YOU
NOZINIT	NOSE IN IT
NUINUU	KNEW I KNEW YOU
NUINUYU	KNEW I KNEW YOU
NUKLHED	KNUCKLEHEAD
NICENEZ	NICE N EASY
NGINEAR	ENGINEER
NOMYSYZ	KNOW MY SIZE
NOT2BCN	NOT TO BE SEEN
NOTIFIC	NO IF I SEE
NJOYIT	ENJOY IT
NJOYIT2	INJOY IT TOO
NOCMEUP	BRITISH TERMINOLOGY
NITPIKR	KNIT PICKER
NORGRTZ	NO REGRETS
NORGRTS	NO REGRETS
NVRFEAR	NEVER FEAR
NOBDRSZ	NO BED ROSES
NOPL2GO	NO PLACE TO GO
NICENEZ	NICE N EASY

"O"

OK4NOW	OK FOR NOW
OKIFUDO	OK IF YOU DO
OKUCIT	OK YOU SEE IT
OKUCIT2	OK YOU SEE IT TOO
OKUDONT	OK YOU DON'T
OKCHICK	OK CHICK
OKCHIX	OK CHICKS
OFFOFIT	OFF OF IT
OK43	OK FOR THREE
OHWELL	OH WELL
OK46	OK FOR SIX
OK4SIX	OK FOR SIX
OUTLAWD	OUTLAWED
ODRZBAD	ODORS BAD
ODRSBAD	ODORS BAD
OBOYRU	OH BOY ARE YOU
OHBOYRU	OH BOY ARE YOU

OK4U	OK FOR YOU
OK4YU	OK FOR YOU
OK4U2	OK FOR YOU TO
OK4U2B1	OK FOR YOU TO BE ONE
OK4ME2	OK FOR ME TO
OSHUCKS	OH SHUCKS
OSHUCKZ	OH SHUCKS
OHSAYIT	OH SAY IT
OKBYME	OK BY ME
OKBYME2	OK BY ME TOO
OUTSOLD	OUT SOLD
OKBUYME	OK BUY ME
ODORIT	ODOR IT
ODORIT2	ODOR IT TOO
ODORME	ODOR ME
ODOREME	ADORE ME
OKC2IT	OK SEE TO IT
OKUDONT	OK YOU DON'T
ONCEUDO	ONCE YOU DO
ONCEIDO	ONCE I DO
ONTHERZ	ON THE RISE
ONTHERS	ON THE RISE
ODZR321	ODDS ARE THREE TO ONE
OVEREZE	OVER EASY
OUTRAYJ	OUTRAGE
OUTRAJD	OUTRAGED
OYSTRMN	OYSTERMAN
OVRBRG	OVERBEARING

OVERBRG	OVERBEARING
OVRBRNG	OVERBEARING
OSPREYS	OSPREYS
OSPREYZ	OSPREYS
ONEHYIQ	ONE HIGH IQ
ODRETRS	ODOR EATERS
ODRETRZ	ODOR EATERS
OFUDGE	OH FUDGE
OHFUDGE	OH FUDGE
OKMYEYE	OK MY EYE
O4PTZSK	OH FOR PETES SAKE
OLIMPIA	OLYMPIA
OVRBORD	OVERBOARD
OLDANTQ	OLD ANTIQUE
OLANTIQ	OLD ANTIQUE
OURGLAS	HOURGLASS
OHYUKID	OH YOU KID
ONLYASK	ONLY ASK
OMELETS	OMELETS
OMELETZ	OMELETS
ORCHIDS	ORCHIDS
ORCKIDS	ORCHIDS
ORCKIDZ	ORCHIDS
ORIGAMI	ART OF FOLDING PAPER
OOYGORD	OUT OF OU GJORD
ODODUMB	OH SO DUMB
OSONICE	OH SO NICE
OSOCUTE	OH SO CUTE

OSOTRUE	OH SO TRUE
OURKIDS	OUR KIDS
OURKIDZ	OUR KIDS
ONUDLES	OH NOODLES
ONUDLEZ	OH NOODLES
ORNGJUS	ORANGE JUICE
ORNGJCZ	ORANGE JUICE
ORNGJCE	ORANGE JUICE
OBALONE	OH BALONEY
OLDMAID	OLD MAID
OLDMADE	OLD MAID
OVLTEEN	OVALTINE
OVLTYN	OVALTINE
OVELTYN	OVALTINE
OVALTYN	OVALTINE
OPTCYEL	OPTIC YELLOW
OFF2RCZ	OFF TO RACES
OLBLSTR	OLD BLISTER
OHBLSYU	OH BLESS YOU
OBLESSU	OH BLESS YOU
OKIFUDO	OK IF YOU DO
OKIFIDO	OK IF I DO
OUDLOV2	OH YOU'D LOVE TO
OYUDLV2	OH YOU'D LOVE TO
OKTOPUS	OCTOPUS
OKTOEPS	OCTOPUS
OKTOWPS	OCTOPUS
OUTASYT	OUT A SIGHT

VANITY PLATE EXPRESSIONS

OUTAMND	OUT A MIND
OPNYRIZ	OPEN YOUR EYES
OPNYRHT	OPEN YOUR HEART
OLFOSIL	OLD FOSSILL
OLBLSTR	OLD BLISTER
OPLISTR	OLD BLISTER
OTHELES	NONE THE LESS
OISZERO	"O" IS ZERO
OUTAMNY	OUT A MONEY
ONT2RLTY	ON TO REALITY
OUTASGT	OUT A SIGHT
OUTASYT	OUT A SIGHT
OUTAMND	OUT A MIND

"P"

PLAITUP	PLAY IT UP
PROCDOC	PROCTOLOGY DOCTOR
PLUMBME	CARPENTER TALK
PLAONIT	PLAY ON IT
PAINTIT	PAINT IT
PLUGIT	PLUGIT
PLUGIT2	PLUG IT TOO
PAZBAD	PAYS BAD
PAYSBAD	PAYS BAD
PAYDAYZ	PAYDAYS
PUNCHME	PUNCH ME
PCHNJDY	PUNCH N JUDY
PANOZIT	PA KNOWS IT
PICPERT	PICTURE PERFECT
PICPURF	PICTURE PERFECT
PERFPIC	PERFECT PICTURE
PURFPIC	PERFECT PICTURE

PRA4ME	PRAY FOR ME
PEEK4ME	PEEK FOR ME
PEEK4IT	PEEK FOR IT
PETNPUR	PET N PURR
PITITIS	PIT IT IS
PITITIZ	PIT IT IS
PARTZIN	PARTIES IN
PAPERIT	PAPER IT
PCBYPC	PIECE BY PIECE
PZBYPZ	PIECE BY PIECE
PETESA	PIZZA
PYNXPNK	PINKS PINK
POPZIN2	POPS IN TOO
POPSIN2	POPS IN TOO
POPSIN	POPS IN
POPZIN	POPS IN
PEAZNQZ	PEAS N QUES
PZANQZ	PEAS N QUES
PASNBY	PASSIN BY
PASYNBY	PASSIN BY
PASNBY2	PASSIN BY TOO
PASITON	PASS IT ON
PASMEBY	PASS ME BY
PLZSPUP	PLEASE SPEAK UP
PURQLTY	PURE QUALITY
PLZTAK1	PLEASE TAKE ONE
PINXPNK	PINKS PINK
PIGNPOK	PIG IN POKE

PIGNPK	PIG IN POKE
PRVMYPT	PROVE MY POINT
PLESEME	PLEASE ME
PLEZME	PLEASE ME
POOPDEK	POOP DECK
POLYSTR	POLYESTER
PLESTER	POLYESTER
PJAMAZ	PAJAMAS
PAJAMAZ	PAJAMAS
PANTSHD	PANTS HARD
POLKADT	POLKA DOT
POPYCOX	POPPY COCKS
PLASTRD	PLASTERED
PELICAN	PELICAN
PUZZLER	PUZZLER
PUFADER	SNAKE
PIEFACE	PIE FACE
PYTHON	SNAKE
PRKIPYN	PORCUPINE
POP1OFF	POP ONE OFF
POP14ME	POP ONE FOR ME
POPGZWZ	POP GOES WEASEL
PECEMKR	PEACE MAKER
PEKABOO	PEEK A BOO
POLARUS	POLARUS
PROPWSH	PROP WASH
PAZMEBY	PASS ME BY
PSTMEBY	PASS ME BY

PUNYBGR	PUNY BUGGER
PNYBUGR	PUNY BUGGER
PTLOVER	PART-TIME LOVER
PSTHEYU	PST HEY YOU
PAWS4IT	PAUSE FOR IT
PAWZ4IT	PAUSE FOR IT
PAZADOC	PAWS A DOCTOR
PAZASEC	PAUSE A SECOND
POPSICO	POPCICLE
POPSYCL	POPCICLE
PATHETC	PATHETIC
PLASURE	PLEASURE
PLESURE	PLEASURE
PULLUP	SAME FW & BW
PUZZLED	PUZZLED
PADLWHL	PADDLE WHEEL
PLZSQK	PLEASE SQUEAK
PLZSQEK	PLEASE SQUEAK
PKZPEAK	PIKES PEAK
PKZPEEK	PIKES PEAK
PAINTER	PAINTER
PLUMBER	PLUMBER
PRINTER	PRINTER
PALICE	PALACE
PULLTOY	PULL TOY
PUSH TOY	PUSH TOY
PILFERD	PILFERED
PLRZMYN	PLEASURES MINE

PTYDMYN	PETTY DAMNED QUIET
POWERLS	POWERLESS
PB4UGO	PEE BEFORE YOU GO
PRUFPOZ	PROOF POSITIVE
PADLOKZ	PADLOCKS
PADLOX	PADLOCKS
PADALOX	PADLOCKS
PATENTS	PATENTS
PRSONLY	PERSONALLY
PRSNLY	PERSONALLY
PERSNLY	PERSONALLY
PNUTBTR	PEANUT BUTTER
PNTBUTR	PEANUT BUTTER
POPCOBA	POPCORN BALLS
POPTCORN	POPPED CORN
PUZLEME	PUZZLE ME
PRKNBNZ	PORK N BEANS
PCHEZ	PEACHES
PEEZAH	PIZZA
PEEZUH	PIZZA
PEETZUH	PIZZA
POT8TOZ	POTATOS
PT8TOCP	POTATO CHIP
PLAYGAL	PLAY GAL
PLAYBOY	PLAY BOY
PTHETIC	PATHETIC
PAYPRBY	PAPERBOY
PAPRBOY	PAPERBOY

PTYCLHA	PRETTY COOL HUH
PTYANML	PARTY ANIMAL
PAIDFOR	PAID FOR
PAID4	PAID FOR
PRADICE	PARADISE
PRADYCE	PARIDISE
PAYSHNZ	PATIENCE
PISTLPT	PISTOL PETE
PSTLPT	PISTOL PETE
PISTOLP	PISTOL PETE
PRBLUNS	PROBLEMS
PRBLUMZ	PROBLEMS
PROBLMS	PROBLEMS
PROBLMZ	PROBLEMS
PAZADOC	PAWS A DOCTOR
PAZASEC	PAUSE A SECOND
PUSHME	PUSH ME
PODRAZ	SAN DIEGO PADRES
POPEYE	POPEYE
PEEP4ME	PEEP FOR ME
PURR4ME	PURR FOR ME
PLUNGER	PLUNGER
PRACHUT	PARACHUTE
PRASHUT	PARACHUTE
PORKCHOP	PORKCHOP
POT8OCH	POTATO CHIP
POT8O	POTATO
POT8OCH	POTATO CHIP

PATIGER	PAPPA TIGER
POINTER	DOG
POODLE	DOG
PKPCKAT	PINK PUSSY CAT
PKPYKAT	PINK PUSSY CAT
PKPYCAT	PINK PUSSY CAT
POKATLA	POCATELLA IDAHO
POKATELA	POCATELLA IDAHO
PERFECT	PERFECT
PRFCTN	PERFECTION
PERFCTN	PERFECTION
PR2DRW2	PAIR TO DRAW TO
PEKATME	PEEK AT ME
PIGSEAR	PIGS EAR
PIGZEAR	PIGS EAR
PIDJUNS	PIGEONS
PIDJUNZ	PIGEONS
PLZASAP	PLEASE ASAP
POUD2B	PROUD TO BE
PRFCTLV	PERFECT LOVE
PRFTLVR	PERFECT LOVER
PAYBYCK	PAY BY CHECK
PR2DR2	PAIR TO DRAW TOO
PLYEARS	PLIERS
PRE1ODR	PRETINDER
PAT1OT	PATENT
PYPFITR	PIPEFITTER
PITCH4K	PITCHFORK

PLAY2IT	PLAY TO IT
PITYPOT	PITTY POT POO
PTPOTPU	PITTY POT POO
PTLOVER	PART TIME LOVER
PUSHOVR	PUSHOVER
PATYKAK	PATTY CAKE
PICOLTR	PICK OF LITTER
PRADICE	PAIR OF DICE
PTYTRND	PARTY TRAINED

"Q"

QUITIT	QUIT IT
QYETPLZ	QUIET PLEASE
QYETMOM	QUIET MOM
QYETYOU	QUIET YOU
QYETDAD	QUIET DAD
QYETSIS	QUIET SIS
QYEYU	QUIET YOU
QYETYU	QUIET YOU
QYET4ME	QUIET FOR ME
QBALSIN	QUE BALLS IN
QBALZIN	QUE BALLS IN
QTRSWRT	QUARTERS WORTH
QTRZWRT	QUARTERS WORTH
QUACKIN	CRACK IN
QTZROK	CUTIES ARE OK
QTZRNYC	CUTIES ARE NICE
QUEENBE	QUEEN BEE

QUEENB	QUEEN BEE
QUEEN2B	QUEEN TO BE
QTPIE	CUTIE PIE
QTCUTIE	CUTIE CUTIE
QTTYKE	CUTE TYKE
QTRPNDR	QUARTER POUNDER
QUAKNUP	CRACKIN UP
QYTALKN	QUIT TALKIN
QCUMBER	CUCUMBER
QCUMBUR	CUCUMBER
QTYRBTC	QUIT YOUR BITCHIN
QTYRBCN	QUIT YOUR BITCHIN
QUEZEZE	SQUEEZE EASY
QUEZEME	SQUEEZE ME
QPDOLL	CUPIE DOLL
QPEDOLL	CUPIE DOLL
QPDOLLZ	CUPIE DOLLS
QUAKTUP	CRACKED UP
QTBTUGL	CUTE BUT UGLY
QTBUTUG	CUTE BUT UGLY
QUTUNOT	CUTE BUT NOT
QTUKNOT	CUTE BUT NOT
QTUARNT	CUTE YOU AREN'T
QTBUGS	CUTE BUGS
QTBUGZ	CUTE BUGS
QTHUTRS	CUTE HOOTERS
QTHUTRZ	CUTE HOOTERS
QYTENUF	QUITE ENOUGH

QUESEEN	CUISINE
QUEZEEN	CUISINE
QTNSASY	CUTE N SASSY
QYTAGAL	QUITE A GAL
QYETPLZ	QUIET PLEASE
QYETPLS	QUIET PLEASE
QYTAGUY	QUITE A GUY
QYTABIT	QUITE A BIT

"R"

RUINME2	RUIN ME TOO
RUINME	RUIN ME
ROLOVRB	ROLL OVER BETHOVEN
RWEINIT	ARE WE IN IT
RU1TOO	ARE YOU ONE TOO
RU12	ARE YOU ONE TOO
RYUONE2	ARE YOU ONE TOO
RUMAD2	ARE YOU MAD TOO
RUMAD	ARE YOU MAD
RYUMAD	ARE YOU MAD
RYOUMAD	ARE YOU MAD
ROCKDOC	ROCK DOC
RUSICK	ARE YOU SICK
RYUSICK	ARE YOU SICK
RUSICK2	ARE YOU SICK TOO
REDZHOT	RED'S HOT
RUNBYME	RUN BY ME

RULEIT	RULE IT
REDBLUD	RED BLOOD
RESLME	WRESTLE ME
RESLEME	WRESTLE ME
RESLME2	WRESTLE ME TOO
RYT2IT	RIGHT TO IT
RITE2IT	RIGHT TO IT
RIOTRUN	RIOT RUN
RUNHARD	RUN HARD
RWE2B1	ARE WE TO BE ONE
RWE2B12	ARE WE TO BE ONE TOO
RUUPTOO	ARE YOU UP TOO
RUUP2IT	ARE YOU UP TOO IT
RUUPTWO	ARE YOU UP TOO
ROXROK	ROCKS ARE OK
ROXRROX	ROCKS ARE ROCKS
ROLLOVR	ROLL OVER
ROLOVER	ROLL OVER
ROLLIT	ROLL IT
ROL14ME	ROLL ONE FOR ME
RUHAPPY	ARE YOU HAPPY
RU2TALL	ARE YOU TOO TALL
RUMIFT	ARE YOU MIFFED
RUSMALL	ARE YOU SMALL
RUSTBKT	RUST BUCKET
RSTBUKT	RUST BUCKET
R8BLZOK	ARE EIGHT BALLS OK
RUINIT	ARE YOU IN IT

RUROKIN	ARE YOU ROCKIN
RUROTIN	ARE YOU ROTTEN
RUEVRIN	ARE YOU EVER IN
RATZRIN	RATS ARE IN
ROXTOIT	ROCKS TO IT
ROCKZ2T	ROCKS TO IT
ROX2IT	ROCKS TO IT
ROX2IT2	ROCKS TO IT TOO
ROXRIN	ROCKS ARE IN
ROXRIN2	ROCKS ARE IN TOO
RUREADY	ARE YOU READY
RUREDDY	ARE YOU READY
RUREDDE	ARE YOU READY
RUREDY	ARE YOU READY
RUREDY2	ARE YOU READY TOO
RUEVRIT	ARE YOU EVER IT
RUWHTUR	ARE YOU WHAT YOU ARE
RU4REEL	ARE YOU FOR REAL
RUSTKUP	ARE YOU STUCK UP
RUSTSIN	RUSTS IN
RUSTZIN	RUSTS IN
RUGAYM	ARE YOU GAME
RYUGAYM	ARE YOU GAME
REALTYT	REAL TIGHT
REELTYT	REAL TIGHT
RESURCH	RESEARCH
RUWIERD	ARE YOU WEIRD
RDMYIZ	READ MY EYES

RDMYLPS	READ MY LIPS
RDMYLPZ	READ MY LIPS
REDZRED	REDS RED
RZITZIN	ARE ZITS IN
RZITZIT	ARE ZITS IT
ROXNSOX	ROCKS N SOCKS
RUTRUE2	ARE YOU TRUE TOO
RUTRU2	ARE YOU TRUE TOO
RZRHOTR	OURS ARE HOTTER
RULEROF	RULER OF
RULROV1	RULER OF ONE
RUOK2ME	ARE YOU OK TO ME
RAMBLIN	RAMBLIN
RUN4LYF	RUN FOR LIFE
REST4ME	REST FOR ME
RUSERUS	ARE YOU SERIOUS
RUWETYT	ARE YOU WET YET
RLMEOVR	ROLL ME OVER
RNZCIT	REG NURSES SEE IT
RNZFLIT	REG NURSES FEEL IT
RNZDOIT	REG NURSES DO IT
RNZCAN	REG NURSES CAN
RNZCAN2	REG NURSES CAN TOO
RNZLVIT	REG NURSES LOVE IT
RNZSQIT	REG NURSES SQUEEZE IT
RUINDME	RUINED ME
ROTIRON	WROUGHT IRON
RAINZIN	RAINS IN

RNDNRND	ROUND N ROUND
RWEWYZE	ARE WE WISE
RWEWIZE	ARE WE WISE
RWEWISE	ARE WE WISE
RYT2IT	RIGHT TO IT
RDSKYNS	REDSKINS
RAYDRS	RAIDERS
RDSKYNZ	REDSKINS
RAYDRZ	RAIDERS
RALRODE	RAILROAD
RU2FAST	ARE YOU TOO FAST
RYNKLME	WRINKLE ME
RUALUSR	ARE YOU A LOSER
RUALUZR	ARE YOU A LOSER
RUREDHD	ARE YOR A RED HEAD
RUAFINK	ARE YOU A FINK
RUAFYNK	ARE YOU A FINK
RESYKO	RECYCLE
RESYCLE	RECYCLE
RESYCLG	RECYCLING
REVERQY	RIVER QUAY
RUMPRST	RUMP ROAST
ROMEO	ROMEO
ROWMEOW	ROMEO
ROMNJUL	ROMEO N JULIET
RNGOSTR	RINGO STARR
ROWCHEZ	ROACHES
RACER	RACER

RLROFLV	RULER OF LOVE
RONGWMN	WRONG WOMAN
RESYKOL	RECYCLE
RUTCANL	ROOT CANAL
RTCANAL	ROOT CANAL
RTECANL	ROOT CANAL
RELION1	RELY ON ONE
RU4KEPS	ARE YOU FOR KEEPS
RU4KEPZ	ARE YOU FOR KEEPS
RTYR2GY	RETIRE TO GOODYEAR
REDRSTR	RED ROOSTER
RAGDOLL	RAGDOLL
RAGDOLS	RAGDOLL S
RAGDOLZ	RAGDOLLS
RACECAR	SAME FW & BW
RADAR	SAME FW & BW
REDDER	SAME FW & BW
REFER	SAME FW & BW
REPAPER	SAME FW & BW
RUALUSH	ARE YOU A LUSH
RUAYOYO	ARE YOU A YOYO
RUAFOOL	ARE YOU A FOOL
RUADORK	ARE YOU A DORK
RUACREP	ARE YOU A CREEP
RUAFROG	ARE YOU A FROG
RELAXME	RELAX ME
RU4REAL	ARE YOU FOR REAL
REPOWRD	REPOWERED

REGNURS	REGISTERED NURSE
RANCHER	RANCHER
RACKUN	RACCOON
RACHUNE	RACCOON
RACKOON	RACCOON
RUMBLER	RUMBLER
RHUBARB	RHUBARB
ROTNKID	ROTTIN KID
RUFMEUP	ROUGH ME UP
RELSICK	REAL SICK
REDROSE	RED ROSE
RABLRSR	RABBLE ROUSER
RABLRZR	RABBLE ROUSER
RUNOTY	ARE YOU NAUGHTY
RUKNOTY	ARE YOU NAUGHTY
RUCURLE	ARE YOU CURLIE
RUMYTYP	ARE YOU MY TYPE
ROLROTZ	ROLLER OATS
RELSNPR	REAL SNAPPER
RARN2GO	RARIN TO GO
RUGILTY	ARE YOU GUILYT
RUMNCOK	RUM AND COKE
RESUMES	RESUMES
REZUMEZ	RESUMES
ROKGRDNS	ROCK GARDENS
RSEZRED	ROSES RED
RENCHES	WRENCHES
RENCHEZ	WRENCHES

RASINZ	RAISINS
RAZINZ	RAISINS
REDHEAT	REDHEAT
RWENUTS	ARE WE NUTS
RWENUTZ	ARE WE NUTS
RLPORKR	REAL PORKER
RAINBOW	RAINBOW
RAZRBAK	RAZORBACK
RDRURNR	ROADRUNNER
RDRUNNR	ROADRUNNER
RUMYDMY	RUMMY DUMMY
RMYDUMY	RUMMY DUMMY
RMYNOK	ARE MINE OK
ROAR4ME	ROAR FOR ME
ROWSTBF	ROAST BEEF
RMADILO	ARMADILLO
RPMLOW	RPMLOW
RVRRFTR	RIVER RAFTER
RAYD8TR	RADIATOR
RELAYME	RELAY ME
RELDUZE	REAL DOOZIE
RAYDOPR	RADIO OPERATOR
RUFORRL	ARE YOU FOR REAL
RUMXTUP	ARE YOU MIXED UP
RUCNFZD	ARE YOU CONFUSED
RUCNFSD	ARE YOU CONFUSED
RUYUCKE	ARE YOU YUCKIE
RUYUKKE	ARE YOU YUCKIE

RUYUKEY	ARE YOU YUCKIE
RGYLSOX	ARGYLE SOX
RELYOYO	REAL YOYO
RUMYTYP	ARE YOU MY TYPE
RUABUGR	ARE YOU A BUGGER
RYNKLES	WRINKLES
RYNKLEZ	WRINKLES
RNKYDNK	RINKY DINK
RESQUME	RESCUE ME
RESQME2	RESCUE ME TOO
RESQMYN	RESCUE MINE
RUAQUTR	ARE YOU A QUITTER
REALHIP	REAL HIP
ROTN2CR	ROTTEN TO CORE
RELEAFT	RELIEVED
RELEAST	RELEASED
RUFZCOB	ROUGH AS COB
RUMYDAD	ARE YOU MY DAD
RUASGRD	ARE YOU A SUGAR DADDY
ROPEDIN	ROPED IN
RU2XCTG	ARE YOU TOO EXCITING
RU2DULL	ARE YOU TOO DULL
RU2UGLY	ARE YOU TOO UGLY
RUTAKEN	ARE YOU TAKEN
REELNUT	FISHERMAN TALK
RUNICER	ARE YOU NICER
RONG14U	WRONG ONE FOR YOU
RISKAY1	RISKY ONE

RISKEY1	RISKY ONE
RNDROBN	ROUND ROBIN
REALQTE	REAL CUTIE
REELQTE	REAL CUTIE
REELQT	REAL CUTE
REALQT	REAL CUTE
RNGMYBL	RING MY BELL
RUAWYNR	ARE YOU A WINNER
RUAWINR	ARE YOU A WINNER
RUAYNR	ARE YOU A WINNER
RUAYNR2	ARE YOU A WINNER TOO
RUCNFSD	ARE YOU CONFUSED
RUCNFZD	ARE YOU CONFUSED
RUUGLEE	ARE YOU UGLY
RODNOC	CONDOR BACKWARDS
RUTHRU	ARE YOU THROUGH
RSONIST	ARSONIST
RSONIZ	ARE SON IS
RUMY1DL	ARE YOU MY ONE DOLL
REFRGR8	REFRIGERATE
REGENR8	REGENERATE
REGNR8	REGENERATE
RMD2HLT	ARMED TO HILT
RIKSHAW	RICKSHAW
RICSHAW	RICKSHAW
RUABUM	ARE YOU A BUM
RUABUMR	ARE YOU A BUMMER
RESL14U	RUSTLE ONE FOR YOU

RUSLME	RUSTLE ME
RUSLME1	RUSTLE ME ONE
RUSLME2	RUSTLE ME TOO
RAMBULL	RAMBO
RAMBOW	RAMBO
ROWPTIN	ROPED IN

"S"

SOOTSME	SUITS ME
SOOTZME	SUITS ME
STARDAT	STARRED AT
STUDDED	STUDDED
SLIPJIG	SLIPJIG
STUPID	STUPID
SURFSIN	SURFS IN
SURFZIN	SURFS IN
SPYDERS	SPIDERS
SPYDERZ	SPIDERS
SPYDURS	SPIDERS
SPYDURZ	SPIDERS
SPEARIT	SPIRIT
SPIRIT	SPIRIT
SPAGETI	SPAGHETTI
SKYLYT	SKYLITE
SKYLYTS	SKYLITES

SKYLYTZ	SKYLITES
STARBST	STARBURST
STARBRT	STARBRIGHT
SYRINGE	SYRINGE
SKYLARK	SKYLARK
SUZAFON	SOUZAPHONE
SNAPPER	SNAKE
SDACRKR	SODA CRACKER
SKINBUF	SKIN BUFF
SKIBUMB	SKI BUMB
SAFNSND	SAFE N SOUND
SHUSALZ	SHOE SALES
SUESHEE	JAPANESE FOOD
SKINE1	SKINNY ONE
SKYNE1	SKINNY ONE
STAKULE	STAY COOL
STACULE	STAY COOL
STAKUL	STAY COOL
SHOMEUP	SHOW ME UP
SURBNYC	SURE BE NICE
SKULPTR	SCULPTOR
SEEATL	SEATTLE
SEATL	SEATTLE
SLORYDR	SLOW RIDER
SLOMUVR	SLOW RIDER
SNOWJOB	SNOW JOB
SNOJOB	SNOW JOB
SNOWSOK	SNOWS OK

SNOWZOK	SNOWS OK
SHOTROD	SHOT ROD
SCREWUP	SCREW UP
SOLDOUT	SOLD OUT
SOBEIT	SO BE IT
SEWBEIT	SO BE IT
SHOTUP	SHOT UP
SHUTUP	SHOT UP
SPEEDUP	SPEED UP
SKINUT	SKI NUT
SKINUTS	SKI NUTS
SKINUTZ	SKI NUTS
SKYNUT	SKY NUT
SKYNUTS	SKY NUTS
SKYNUTZ	SKY NUTS
STYNKS	STINKS
STYNKZ	STINKS
SAWITUP	SAW IT UP
SUPRCHF	SUPER CHIEF
SCRAPIT	SCRAP IT
SINSRIT	SINS ARE IT
SINZRIT	SINS ARE IT
SNZR4ME	SINS ARE FOR ME
STOMPIT	STOMP IT
SNOWSIN	SNOWS IN
SNOWZIN	SNOWS IN
SNOWDIN	SNOWED IN
SKI4ME	SKI FOR ME

SKI4ME	SKI FOR ME TOO
SADSACK	SAD SACK
SADSAX	SAK SACK
SEXISIN	SEX IS IN
SEXIZIN	SEX IS IN
STAGRME	STAGGER ME
SKNYDPR	SKINNY DIPPER
STUFFED	STUFFED
STUFFT	STUFFED
SINCRLY	SINCERELY
SWIMOUT	SWIM OUT
SKYDIVR	SKYDIVER
SHEZMYN	SHE'S MINE
SEXYLDY	SEXY LADY
STANDUP	STANDUP
SITDOWN	SITDOWN
STARS2U	STARS TO YOU
STARZ2U	STARS TO YOU
SUNYDAZ	SUNNY DAYS
STIXRIN	STICKS ARE IN
SLYFOX	SLY FOX
SELLIT	SELL IT
SHOMETO	SHOW ME TOO
SHOME1	SHOW ME ONE
SHOME12	SHOW ME ONE TOO
SHOBIZ	SHOW BIZ
SHOWBIZ	SHOW BIZ
SCOOTBY	SCOOT BY

SCOOTIN	SCOOT IN
SLOPYME	SLOPPY ME
SICKUM	SICKUM
SICUM	SICKUM
STROKER	STROKER
STROKUR	STROKER
SHUUCKZ	SHUCKS
SHUUCKS	SHUCKS
SHUUKS	SHUCKS
SHUUKZ	SHUCKS
SLEPTIN	SLEPT IN
SNOKRD	SNOCKERED
SNOOKER	POOL GAME
SNOOKUR	POOL GAME
SILENT1	SILENT ONE
SYLENT1	SILENT ONE
SHOWMEY	SHOW ME WHY
SHOMEY	SHOW ME WHY
SHOEME	SHOW ME
SHOEME1	SHOW ME ONE
SHOEME2	SHOW ME TOO
SHOME	SHOW ME
SHAWLWE	SHALL WE
STRUTIN	STRUTTIN
STALAYT	STAY LATE
SUNAGUN	SON OF A GUN
SHFTRIN	SHIFTER IN
SHIFTER	SHIFTER

STAFFIT	STAFF IT
SISTUMS	SYSTEMS
SISTUMZ	SYSTEMS
SYSTMOK	SYSTEM OK
SAWUIZ	SAW YOU EYES
SAWYUIZ	SAW YOU EYES
SKPTOUT	SKIPPED OUT
SKPTOVER	SKIPPED OVER
STICMUP	STICKEM UP
STIKMUP	STICKEM UP
SNEEKY1	SNEAKY ONE
SNEEKEY	SNEAKY
SNOSHUZ	SNOWSHOES
SNOSHOE	SNOWSHOE
SNOSHOO	SNOWSHOE
SNOWSHU	SNOWSHOE
STMYMOU	SHUT MY MOUTH
SHTMYMO	SHUT MY MOUTH
SEETOIT	SEE TO IT
SEE2IT2	SEE TO IT TOO
SITONIT	SIT ON IT
SEXPOET	SEX POET
SITONME	SIT ON ME
SKYNDWN	SKINDOWN
SKNEDIP	SKINNY DIP
SKNDEEP	SKIN DEEP
SOXRON	SOCKS ARE ON
SOXRIN	SOCKS ARE IN

STNKYSX	STINKY SOCKS
SOXUGLY	SOCKS UGLY
STYNKY1	STINKY ONE
SKYNZOK	SKINS OK
SKYNSOK	SKINS OK
SKYNZIN	SKINS IN
SKINZIN	SKINS IN
SUITZME	SUITS ME
SYKODOC	PSYCHO DOC
STYNKER	STINKER
STINGKR	STINKER
SINSBAD	SINS BAD
SINZBAD	SINS BAD
SYNZBAD	SINS BAD
SLIPTIN	SLIPPED IN
SOPRANO	SOPRANO
SUNYDAZ	SUNNY DAYS
STRANIT	STRAIN IT
STALUVR	STAY LOVER
STALVRZ	STAY LOVERS
SUGRDDY	SUGAR DADDY
SYSTMZR	SYSTEMS ARE
SIGHZME	SIZE ME
SYZMEUP	SIZE ME UP
SIXRHDZ	SIX ARE HALF DOZEN
SINFANE	SYNPHONY
SYNFUNE	SYNPHONY
SYNFONE	SYNPHONY

SKYLYNR	SKYLINER
SUCRDIN	SUCKERED IN
SERCHME	SEARCH ME
SOPEBOX	SOAP BOX
SOWPBOX	SOAP BOX
SEWPBOX	SOAP BOX
STKYSKR	STINKY SUCKER
SUGRPLM	SUGAR PLUM
SAWSEEG	SAUSAGE
SLEPEIZ	SLEEPY EYES
SLEEPYI	SLEEPY EYE
SNAKEIZ	SNAKE EYES
SFTSKYN	SOFT SKIN
SQUARIT	SQUARE IT
SQITOFF	SQUARE IT OFF
SEA2IT	SEE TO IT
SEETOIT	SEE TO IT
SKI2IT	SKI TO IT
SING4ME	SING FOR ME
SEWITBE	SO IT BE
SEWBIT	SO BE IT
SEWBEIT	SO BE IT
SWETHOG	SWEAT HOG
SYMPLME	SIMPLE ME
SMPLYME	SIMPLY ME
SHUDOC	SHOE REPAIRMAN
SHUEDOC	SHOE REPAIRMAN
STNDBAK	STAND BACK

SUPRZME	SURPRISE ME
SCRDSTF	SCARED STIFF
SGTUNSN	SIGHT UNSEEN
SYTUNSN	SIGHT UNSEEN
SQKYCLN	SQUEEKY CLEAN
SNEKERS	SNEAKERS
SNEKERZ	SNEAKERS
SIRJUN	SURGEON
SHARMYN	SHARE MINE
SHARMIN	SHARE MINE
SLPRYGY	SLIPPERY GUY
SUFRWME	SUFFER WITH ME
SQUEZME	SQUEEZE ME
SPACCAS	SPACE CASE
SPACCDT	SPACE CADET
SPACFRK	SPACE FREAK
SCTYDOG	SECURITY DOG
SCTYDOG	SCOTTY DOG
SADENME	SADDEN ME
STRFRYD	STIR FRIED
SCALLOP	SCALLOP
SEASLUG	SEASLUG
SHRIMP	SHRIMP
SPONGE	SPONGE
SHUDBME	SHOULD BE ME
SYKOCMC	SYCO CERAMIC (A CRACKED POT)
SNDOLAR	SAND DOLLAR
SPRYZME	SURPRISE ME

SINCLME	CIRCLE ME
SWTSPUD	SWEET POTATO
SNORKEL	SNORKEL
SNOREKL	SNORKEL
SNICKER	SNICKER
SQUIFFY	SQUIFFY
SAMOSHT	SAME OLD SHIT
SPDSTR	SPEEDSTER
SPEDSTR	SPEEDSTER
SEVENUP	SEVENUP
SOURDOE	SOURDOUGH
STRSTOT	STRESSED OUT
STSTOUT	STRESSED OUT
SUPEERB	SUPERB
SUPURRB	SUPERB
SQYAWKR	SQUAWKER
SQUEALR	SQUEALER
SCIZORS	SCISSORS
SCIZERS	SCISSORS
SCIZURS	SCISSORS
SYZERS	SCISSORS
SUNRYZE	SUNRISE
SPLDRTN	SPOILED ROTTEN
SOFTUCH	SOFT TOUCH
SAFBOTG	SAFE BOATING
SMTBTQT	SMART BUT CUTE
STRESS	STRESS
STUDPRK	STUD POKER

SUNTANZ	SUNTANS
SUNTANS	SUNTANS
SALAME	SALAMI
SALAME	SALAMI
SPINICH	SPINACH
SPINECH	SPINACH
SQUEKUP	SQUEAK UP
SQECPLZ	SQUEAK PLEASE
SPYDRWB	SPIDERWEB
SPDRWEB	SPIDERWEB
SPYDURS	SPYDERS
SPYDURZ	SPYDERS
SNAPTUP	SNAPPED UP
STIKTUP	STICKED UP
SQUIRL	SQUIRREL
SQWERL	SQUIRREL
SHAMPAN	CHAMPAGNE
SHMPAYN	CHAMPAGNE
SRQLAYT	CIRCULATE
SKNYMNY	SKINNY MINNIE
SKNKCBG	SKUNK CABBAGE
SMTQUTE	SMART CUTIE
SAYLBRD	SAILBOARD
SAWBUCK	SAWBUCK
SAUNAS	SAUNAS
SHUFLBD	SHUFFLE BOARD
SHFLBRD	SHUFFLE BOARD
SKATBRD	SKATEBOARD

SKATBDG	SKATEBOARDING
SNEEKRS	SNEAKERS
SNEEKRZ	SNEAKERS
SNEKRS	SNEAKERS
STIFNEK	STIFF NECK
SOURCRM	SOUR CREAM
SOWRCRM	SOUR CREAM
SQUEZME	SQWEEZ ME
SQUAWSH	SQUASH
SHORNUF	SURE ENOUGH
SHURNUF	SURE ENOUGH
SHTSNRT	SHORT SNORT
SPGCHIC	SPRING CHICKEN
SPGCHCN	SPRING CHICKEN
SITNHEN	SITTIN HEN
SUBDVYD	SUBDIVIDE
SUBDUDE	SUBUED
SADSTRY	SAD STORY
SOSILLY	SO LILLY
SUEPIG	SUEY PIG
SOOEPIG	SUEY PIG
STNGRBE	STINGER BEE
SOXNJOX	SOCKS N JOCKS
SCRCROW	SCARECROW
SINBNGL	CINCINATTI BENGALS
SNGALNG	SING A LONG
SALLOME	SALAMI
SASAFRS	SASSAFRASS

SCREAMR	SCREAMER
SNIFFER	SNIFFER
SNIFDOG	SNIFFER DOG
SNORTER	SNORTER
SQUEALR	SQUEALER
SCREAM	SCREAM
SCREECH	SCREECH
SNIF4IT	SNIFF FOR IT
SKYDIVE	SKYDIVE
SAKRACE	SACKRACE
SGRLUMP	SUGAR LUMP
SUGRLMP	SUGAR LUMP
SQUARD2	SQUARED TOO
SATYLYT	SATELLITE
SNUGGLY	SNUGGLY
SPTDOWL	SPOTTED OWL
SRAMONY	CEREMONY
SARAMNY	CEREMONY
SANHOSE	SAN JOSE, CALIF
SANHOZE	SAN JOSE, CALIF
SCHNAPS	SCHNAPPS
SCHNAPZ	SCHNAPPS
SLPNBUF	SLEEP IN BUFF
SYTCING	SIGHTSEEING
SAFTNUT	SAFETY NUT
SLVRLNG	SILVER LINING
SCULNCB	SKULL N CROSSBONES
SUMRTYM	SUMMERTIME

VANITY PLATE EXPRESSIONS

SHUDHAV	SHOULD HAVE
SWTNLOW	SWEET N LOW
SITNPGN	SITTIN PIGEON
SITNHEN	SITTIN HEN
SPGCHCN	SPRING CHICKEN
SPRGCHN	SPRING CHICKEN
SWTPARE	SWEET PAIR
SWTPEAR	SWEET PAIR
SWEETPR	SWEET PAIR
SWTPECH	SWEET PEAC
SYTUNSN	SIGHT UNSEEN
SELLDUM	SELDOM
SHUPRSO	SHAPE UP OR SHIP OUT
SITYTE	SIT TIGHT
SITSTIL	SIT STILL
SITTYTE	SIT TIGHT
SITTITE	SIT TIGHT
STUBTYT	READ BACKWARDS
SOWRPUS	SOUR PUSS
SOURPUS	SOUR PUSS
SHINBSR	SHIN BUSTER
SHNBSTR	SHIN BUSTER
SHINOOK	CHINOOK
STRETCH	STRETCH
STREADY	STREET READY
SIRCUT	CIRCUIT
SANANAB	BANANAS BACKWARDS
SNIARB	BRAINS BACKWARDS

STRAMS	SMARTS BACKWARDS
SUINEG	GENIUS BACKWARDS
SASYNQT	SASSY N CUTE
SWSHFTR	SWINGSHIFTER
SHUSH	HUSH UP
SMALFRY	SMALL FRY
SW7DWFS	SNOW WHITE 7 DWARFS
SUNLVR	SUN LOVER
SUNLUVR	SUN LOVER
SQZDOUT	SQUEEZED OUT
SCUTLBT	SCUTTLE BUTT
SQAIRE	SQUARE
SLOMUVR	SLOW MOVER
SLEZE1	SLEEZIES ONE
SHATOE	CHATEAU
SEA2IT	SEE TO IT
SEA2IT2	SEE TO IT TOO
SWEETSU	SWEET SUE
SHOWNTL	SHOW AND TELL

"T"

TRUITIS	TRUE IT IS
TRUITIZ	TRUE IT IS
TOOTHDR	TOOTH DOCTOR
TRY4IT	TRY FOR IT
TAT4TAT	TAT FOR TAT
TOODULL	TOO DULL
TOOOLD2	TOO OLD TOO
THEREIS	THERE IS
THARIZ	THERE IS
THEREIZ	THERE IS
THEYRIS	THERE IS
THEYRIZ	THERE IS
THARSIS	THERE IS
TRYIT	TRY IT
TRYIT2	TRY IT TOO
TISHARD	TIS HARD
TOWME2	TOW ME TOO

TRYITON	TRY IT ON
TUFLUVR	TOUGH LOVER
TYMSMYN	TIMES MINE
TYMZMYN	TIMES MINE
TYTBUNS	TIGHT BUNS
TYTBUNZ	TIGHT BUNS
TYTJUGS	THIGHT JUGS
TYTJUGZ	THIGHT JUGS
TYITON	TIE IT ON
TYDITON	TIED IT ON
TWISTME	TWIST ME
TRUSTME	TRUST ME
TOTUFF2	TOO TOUGH TOO
TYTSHUS	TIGHT SHOES
TYTSHUZ	TIGHT SHOES
TYTWAD	TIGHT WAD
TYTEWAD	TIGHT WAD
TYTGENS	TIGHT JEANS
TYTGENZ	TIGHT JEANS
TAXMAN	TAXMAN
TYDSIN	TIDES IN
TYDZIN	TIDES IN
TIDESIN	TIDES IN
TYDSOUT	TIDES OUT
TYDZOUT	TIDES OUT
TOLOVIS	TO LOVE IS
TOLOVIZ	TO LOVE IS
TOWDOC	PODIATRIST

THYRMYN	THERE MINE
THYRYRS	THERE YOURS
THYRYRZ	THERE YOURS
TWOATEE	TO A "T"
TOOATEE	TO A "T"
TOATEE	TO A "T"
TEZME2	TEASE ME TOO
TEAZME2	TEASE ME TOO
TEEZME2	TEASE ME TOO
TGFBSRW	THANK GOD FOR BEAUTIFUL SINGLE RICH WOMEN
TALK2ME	TALK TO ME
TOTODOG	TOTO'S A DOG
TYITDWN	TIE IT DOWN
TYMEUP	TIE ME UP
TIEDUP	TIED UP
TIEDUP2	TIED UP TOO
TYDUSUP	TIED US UP
THZIZIT	THIS IS IT
TNYHYNY	TINY HINY
TUKITIN	TUCK IT IN
TOEDOC	PODIATRIST
TRI4IT	TRY FOR IT
TRY4IT	TRY FOR IT
TILEMAN	TILEMAN
TYTLIPS	TIGHT LIPS
TYTLIPZ	TIGHT LIPS
TYTBONZ	TIGHT BONES

TITEBNS	TIGHT BONES
TITEBNZ	TIGHT BONES
TYTPTZR	TIGHT PANTS ARE
TRVLSIT	TRAVELS IT
TRVLZIT	TRAVELS IT
TRVLNUT	TRAVEL NUT
TRUBLU	TRUE BLUE
TRUEBLU	TRUE BLUE
TRUBLUE	TRUE BLUE
TVLBYAR	TRAVEL BY AIR
TVLBYCR	TRAVEL BY CAR
TRVBYCR	TRAVEL BY CAR
TOFANCY	TO FANCY
TRUBLIS	TROUBLE IS
TRUBLIZ	TROUBLE IS
TREATME	TREAT ME
TREEME	TREE ME
TAKEME2	TAKE ME TOO
TRUSTME	TRUST ME
TOLDUSO	TOLD YOU SO
TELTRUT	TELL TRUTH
TWOHILT	TO HILT
TREEME2	TRY ME TOO
TURNIT2	TURN IT TOO
TKTCDOC	CLOCK DOCTOR
TZME4IT	TEASE ME FOR IT
TEEZME2	TEASE ME TOO
TOOROOD	TO RUDE

TWOROOD	TO RUDE
TELR4ME	TELL HER FOR ME
TRY4CE	TRY FORCE
TRYFORS	TRY FORCE
TRUBLU	TRUE BLUE
TRYHERS	TRY HERS
TRYHERZ	TRY HERS
TRYSYKO	TRICYCLE
TRYMEON	TRY ME ON
TRYMYSZ	TRY MY SIZE
TIGRPAW	TIGER PAW
TYME4IT	TIE ME FOR IT
TBLWEED	TUMBLEWEED
TIPONIT	TIP ON IT
TORCHLT	TORCHLIGHT
TOKYOJO	TOKYO JOE
TIEBRKR	TIEBREAKER
TYEBRKR	TIEBREAKER
TWOSTEP	TWO STEP
TULIPSR	TWO LIPS ARE
TULIPME	TULIP ME
TULIPZR	TULIPS ARE
TRMYTZ	TERMITES
TRYTS	TERMITES
TURCOYS	TURQUOISE
TURCOYZ	TURQUOISE
TURTLE	TURTLE
TRAYNME	TRAIN ME

TWXNTWN	TWIX N TWEEN
TORQIT	TORQUE IT
TORQUET	TORQUET
TORQME	TORQUE ME
TELMYMA	TELL MY MA
TELMYPA	TELL MY PA
TULOVRS	TWO LOVERS
TULUVRZ	TWO LOVERS
TRULOVRS	TRUE LOVERS
TRULVRZ	TRUE LOVERS
TRY24C	TRY TO FORESEE
TOOTHDR	DENTIST
TUTHSVR	DENTIST
TOOTDR	TRAIN ENGINEER
TOOTSVR	TRAIN COLLECTOR
TOPGUN	TOP GUN
TOPGUNZ	TOP GUNS
TWIDLDE	TWIDDLE DEE
TWIDLDM	TWIDDLE DUM
TACKTUP	TACKED UP
TAPETUP	TAPED UP
THRILLD	THRILLED
TEAPEES	TEEPEES
TEAPEEZ	TEEPEES
TEAPEAS	TEEPEES
TWINPKS	TWIN PEAKS
TWINPKZ	TWIN PEAKS
TODESTL	TOADSTOOL

TWILTYM	TWILIGHT TIME
TRUFLES	TRUFFLES
TRUFLEZ	TRUFFLES
TREDMIL	TREADMILL
TVBORNG	TV'S BORING
TUFFTRK	TOUGH TRUCK
TUFTRUK	TOUGH TRUCK
TYMZSHT	TIMES SHORT
TICTOFF	TICKED OFF
TIKTOFF	TICKED OFF
TRKS4US	TRUCKS FOR US
TRKZ4US	TRUCKS FOR US
TRKSRIN	TRUCKS ARE IN
TRKZRIN	TRUCKS ARE IN
TRTRLVR	TRAVEL TRAILER LOVER
TYTTTTT	TIGHT
TYTOPNG	TIGHT OPENING
TRIFIC	TERRIFIC
TURIFIC	TERRIFIC
TETOTLR	TEATOTTLER
TOBADTO	TOO BAD TOO
TERFYIN	TERRIFING
TYMCLOK	TIME CLOCK
TYMCLOC	TIME CLOCK
TWSTMND	TWISTED MIND
TRUSTME	TRUST ME
TOPHEVY	TOP HEAVY
TYRAID	TIRAIDE

TABYKAT	TABBY CAT
TABBYCT	TABBY CAT
TRNPGNS	TURNIP GREENS
TRNPGNZ	TURNIP GREENS
TYTLTLB	TIGHT LITTLE B
TUTHFRE	TOOTH FAIRY
TWISTER	TWISTER
TRKESUP	TURKEY SOUP
TOE2TOE	TOE TO TOE
TOS2TOS	TOES TO TOES
TOZ2TOZ	TOES TO TOES
TOW2TOW	TOES TO TOES
TOMA2SP	TOMATO SOUP
TOMATOE	TOMATO
TURKYSP	TURKEY SOUP
TURKESP	TURKEY SOUP
TURKEE	TURKEY
TURKEES	TURKEYS
TURKEEZ	TURKEYS
THEBEAV	THE BEAVER
TRU2FRM	TRUE TO FORM
TAKITEZ	TAKE IT EASY
TRQTOFF	TORQUED OFF
TYMEUP	TIE ME UP
TIEMEUP	TIE ME UP
TYMEUP2	TIE ME UP TOO
TITESQZ	TIGHT SQUEEZE
TYTESQZ	TIGHT SQUEEZE

TITEFIT	TIGHT FIT
TYTEFIT	TIGHT FIT
TYTEFYT	TIGHT FIT
TYTYTYT	TIGHT, TIGHT, TIGHT
TOBSOSO	TO BE SOSO
TWSTMND	TWISTED MIND
TUGOWAR	TUG-O-WAR
TATTOOS	TATTOOS
TATTOOZ	TATTOOS
TRILLER	THRILLER
TWITTER	TWITTER
TOOSAWN	TUSCON, ARIZONA
TWOSAN	TUSCON, ARIZONA
TIGERPA	DADDY TIGER
TIGERMA	MOMMY TIGER
TAXIPLZ	TAXI PLEASE
TAXIPLS	TAXI PLEASE
THRLSKR	THRILL SEEKER
TRETOPR	TREETOPPER
TOOTACH	TOOTHACHE
TOOTHAK	TOOTHACHE
TUTHAYK	TOOTHACHE
TFNT2CK	TOUGH NUT TO CRACK
TWASFRS	TWICE AS FRESH
TRFKZPZ	TRAFICS PITZ
TAGALNG	TAGALONG
TAKAHYK	TAKE A HIKE
TRQTOFF	TORQUET OFF

THNKSO	THINK SO
TINKZSO	THINK SO
TUOEMIT	TIMEOUT BACKWARDS
TGIFRID	THANK GOD IT'S FRIDAY
TIWONK1	I KNOW IT BACKWARDS
TLDYASO	TOLD YOU SO
TATLTAL	TATTLE TALK
TATTLER	LOOSE TONGUE
TOWSURG	PODIATRIST
TFNANAZ	TOUGH BANANAS

"U"

URCHIN	URCHIN
ULKALYK	YOU LOOK ALIKE
UDEVILU	YOU DEVIL YOU
UDEVLYU	YOU DEVIL YOU
URZIZQT	YOURS IS CUTE
URSTALN	YOUR STALLIN
UR2ROOD	YOUR TOO RUDE
UR2FAST	YOUR TOO FAST
UAMAZME	YOU AMAZE ME
URAGASR	YOUR A GASSER
UC2IT	YOU SEE TO IT
UC2IT2	YOU SEE TO IT TOO
UBLUIT	YOU BLEW IT
UDBATEM	YOU DEBATEM
UFYTFYN	YOU FIGHT FINE
URUNEK1	YOURE UNIQUE ONE
URUNEK	YOU ARE UNIQUE

ULZRZ2	YOU LOSERS TOO
URLZRZ	YOU ARE LOSERS
UNEEK	UNIQUE
UCITB42	YOU SEE BEFORE TOO
UCB4IDO	YOU SEE BEFOR I DO
U4MYLOV	YOU FOR MY LOVE
UJITRBG	YOU JITTERBUG
UCANB12	YOU CAN BE ONE TOO
UBCOOL	YOU BE COOL
UBKOOL	YOU BE COOL
UBNYC2	YOU BE NICE TOO
UBNC2ME	YOU BE NICE TOO ME
UBMINE	YOU BE MINE
UNYSYCL	UNICYCLE
UNISICL	UNICYCLE
UNYSYKO	UNICYCLE
UNISICL	UNICYCLE
UFOZRIN	UFO'S ARE IN
UOTTOGO	YOU AUTO GO
UAUTOGO	YOU AUTO GO
UCIT4ME	YOU SEE IT FOR ME
UBLEVME	YOU BELIEVE ME
UPFRONT	UP FRONT
UNEED2	YOU NEED TOO
UKNEED2	YOU NEED TOO
UNEEDME	YOU NEED ME
UROKIC	YOU ARE OK I SEE
URSICK	YOUR SICK

UCITZOK	YOU SES IT'S OK
UCITSOK	YOU SEE IT'S OK
UCANIFU	YOU CAN IF YOU
UCANIF	YOU CAN IF
USHOME2	YOU SHOW ME TOO
USHOME1	YOU SHOW ME ONE
URCRAYZ	YOUR CRAZY
URCRAZY	YOUR CRAZY
URGROSS	YOUR GROSS
URZGROZ	YOUR GROSS
URGREAT	YOUR GREAT
UYZUP	YOU WISE UP
UYZUPTO	YOU WISE UP TOO
URGRTST	YOU'R GREATEST
URUINME	YOU RINE ME
UANIMAL	YOU ANIMAL
UANAMIL	YOU ANIMAL
UHAVIT	YOU HAVE IT
UHAVEIT	YOU HAVE IT
UNJOYIT	YOU ENJOY IT
UNJO12	YOU ENJOY ONE TOO
UQUITIT	YOU QUIT IT
UHAVETO	YOU HAVE TOO
UHAVE2	YOU HAVE TOO
U4ME2	YOU FOR ME TOO
UFORME2	YOU FOR ME TOO
UR2CUTE	YOU ARE TOO CUTE
UR2QT41	YOU ARE TOO CUTE FOR ONE

ULCIT2	YOU'LL SEE IT TOO
UWETYET	YOU WET YET
URSOQT	YOU ARE SO CUTE
URSOSO	YOU ARE SOSO
USEWSEW	YOU SOSO
UJITRME	YOU JITTER ME
UCANTB	YOU CAN'T BE
UCANTBE	YOU CAN'T BE
UCMETOO	YOU SEE ME TOO
UCME2	YOU SEE ME TOO
UCANB1	YOU CAN BE ONE
UCANB12	YOU CAN BE ONE TOO
UCANBE1	YOU CAN BE ONE
UTELLME	YOU TELL ME
UHAVE2B	YOU HAVE TO BE
UHAVTOB	YOU HAVE TO BE
UPTOME	UP TO ME
UP2YOU	UP TO YOU
UPTOYOU	UP TO YOU
UPTOU	UP TO YOU
UOUTLAW	YOU OUTLAW
URROTIN	YOU ARE ROTTEN
URNVRIN	YOU ARE NEVER IN
U2WILC	YOU TOO WILL SEE
U2WILLC	YOU TOO WILL SEE
U2WISC1	YOU TOO WILL SEE ONE
U2ROK2	YOU TOO ARE OK TOO
U2ROK2C	YOU TOO ARE OK TO SEE

U2R4IT	YOU TOO ARE FOR IT
U2RAHIT	YOU TOO ARE A HIT
U2R4IT2	YOU TOO ARE FOR IT TOO
USA4ME	U.S.A. FOR ME
USA4ME2	U.S.A. FOR ME TOO
UROUTIT	YOU ARE OUT OF IT
URNTHPY	YOU ARE NOT HAPPY
UBUGMYA	YOU BUG MY A**
UBUGME	YOU BUG ME
UBUGME2	YOU BUG ME TOO
UBUGMYB	YOU BUG MY BUNS
URWHAUR	YOU ARE WHAT YOU ARE
URLEWSR	YOU ARE LOSER
URLOZER	YOU ARE LOSER
ULUZERZ	YOU LOSERS
URLOOSE	YOU ARE LOOSE
UPYURS	UP YOURS
UPYURZ	UP YOURS
UPYURZ2	UP YOURS TOO
UBNICE2	YOU BE NICE TOO
UBNYC21	YOU BE NICE TO ONE
UCAN2B	YOU CAN TOO BE
UCAN2BE	YOU CAN TOO BE
UBORME2	YOU BORE ME TOO
URGD4O	YOU ARE GOOD FOR NOTHING
URAPAYN	YOU ARE A PAIN
URADREM	YOU ARE A DREAM
UR4KEPS	YOU ARE FOR KEEPS

UR4KEPZ	YOU ARE FOR KEEPS
UAKPTWN	YOU A KEPT WOMAN
UOT2NO	YOU OUGHT TO KNOW
UOT2CME	YOU OUGHT TO SEE ME
UGTACME	YOU GOTTA SEE ME
UOT2LOV	YOU OUGHT TO LOVE
UOT2LV	YOU OUGHT TO LOVE
URAGDKD	YOU ARE A GOOD KID
URUNREL	YOU ARE UNREAL
UPRAUAS	UPPER U.S.A.
UZDPRTS	USED PARTS
UZDPRTZ	USED PARTS
URONLY1	YOU ARE ONLY ONE
UTEZME2	YOU TEASE ME TOO
UTEEZME	YOU TEASE ME TOO
UBGMYBU	YOU BUG MY BUTT
UBGMYBT	YOU BUG MY BUTT
UBUZER	YOU BOOZER
UIZOK4U	YOU IS OK FOR YOU
URWIERD	YOUR WEIRD
UGET2ME	YOU GET TO ME
URUNTS	YOU RUNTS
URUNTZ	YOU RUNTS
URUN4ME	YOU RUN FOR ME
UJOG4ME	YOU JOG FOR ME
UXCYTME	YOU EXCITE ME
URXCTNG	YOUR EXCITINE
URTRU2	YOU ARE TRUE TOO

URMYN2	YOU ARE MINE TOO
UTUKRME	YOU TUCKER ME
URNOSEY	YOUR NOSEY
URNOSE1	YOUR NOSEY ONE
URNOSY1	YOUR NOSEY ONE
URBRZRK	YOUR BERSERK
URINDEP	YOUR IN DEEP
URADLYT	YOU'RE A DELIGHT
UKONIKE	YUKON IKE
URUGLY2	YOU ARE UGLY TOO
URMYKND	YOU ARE MY KIND
UR1DRFL	YOU ARE WONDERFUL
URINSTG	YOU ARE INTERESTING
URALOVE	YOU ARE A LOVE
URALOVR	YOU ARE A LOVER
URAKICK	YOU ARE A KICK
URAKISR	YOU ARE A KISSER
URABORE	YOU ARE A BORE
UKNEEK	UNIQUE
U2REXCD	YOU TO ARE EXCUSED
U2RXQZED	YOU TO ARE EXCUSED
URAGASR	YOU'RE A GASSER
ULOSTIT	YOU LOST IT
U2MAYB1	YOU TO MAY BE ONE
UPTMEDR	YOU PATIENT ME DOCTOR
UHITANV	YOU HIT A NERVE
UGLYTRK	UGLY TRICK
USPOILD	YOU SPOILED

UZ2BGUD	USED TO BE GOO
URALUSH	YOU ARE A LUSH
URDIPSO	YOU ARE DIPSO
URSOWST	YOU ARE SOWST
UPINAIR	UP IN AIR
URBERYZ	YOU ARE BERRIES
UTOPIAN	UTOPIAN
URMOOVE	YOUR MOVE
U2BGOOD	YOU TO BE GOOD
UA4RD12	YOU AFFORD ONE TOO
UCANBIF	YOU CAN BE IF
URJSTSO	YOUR JUST SO
UHAVAPR	YOUR HAVE A PROBLEM
UACUTUP	YOU A CUTUP
UNOIDO	YOU KNOW I DO
UNOIDUE	YOU KNOW I DO
UNOIDO2	YOU KNOW I DO TOO
UR2YUNG	YOUR TOO YOUNG
UNEVRNO	YOU NEVER KNOW
URLOUSY	YOUR LOUSY
URLOUZY	YOUR LOUSY
URROUSY	YOUR ROUSY
URROUZY	YOUR ROUSY
UNEVRWL	YOU NEVER WILL
URSOSLY	YOUR SO SLY
URAWINR	YOU ARE A WINNER
UALLCUM	YOU ALL COME
UROKDAD	YOU ARE OK DAD

UROKMOM	YOU ARE OK MOM
UROKSIS	YOU ARE OK SIS
UROKGAL	YOU ARE OK GAL
UROKGUY	YOU ARE OK GUY
UROKBYM	YOU ARE OK BY ME
UNVWASH	UNIV OF WASH
URABAD1	YOU ARE A BAD ONE
URAPYCT	YOU ARE A PUSSY CAT
UAFTRME	YOU AFTER ME
UGARDIT	YOU GUARD IT
UGARDME	YOU GUARD ME
URMYHRO	YOUR MY HERO
URNOBDY	YOUR NOBODY
URMXTUP	YOUR MIXED UP
URCNFSD	YOUR CONFUSED
URCNFZD	YOUR CONFUSED
URMYIDL	YOUR MY IDOL
UGLYDKG	UGLY DUCKLING
ULYD2ME	YOU LIED TO ME
UERKME	YOU ERK ME
USHUDUP	YOU SHUT UP
UDPTME	YOU DUPED ME
UDPTME2	YOU DUPED ME TOO
UCKMEUP	YOU CRACK ME UP
UBUGME	YOU BUG ME
UBUGMYN	YOU BUG MINE
UBUGME2	YOU BUG ME TOO
UCRKTUP	YOU CRACKED UP

UJUSTB1	YOU JUST BE ONE
UERT8ME	YOU IRRITATE ME
UIRTATE	YOU IRRITATE
ULKOK2M	YOU LOOK OK TO ME
URRAANG	YOU RANG
URUPTYT	YOU ARE UPRIGHT
URCRAZY	YOU ARE CRAZY
UP2MYAS	UP TO MY ALL
ULBSORY	YOU'LL BE SORRY
URNGATV	YOU ARE NEGATIVE
UPDCREK	UP THE CRICK
UPDCRIK	UP THE CRICK
URNG4U	YEARNING FOR YOU
UP2MYAS	UP TO MY A**
UNYUNS	ONIONS
UNYONZ	ONIONS
UMISTIT	YOU MISSED IT
URMYIDL	YOU ARE MY IDOL
URMYPET	YOU ARE MY PET
UNOITWO	YOU KNOW IT TOO
URSOBLU	YOU ARE SO BLUE
U2WILLDO	YOU TOO WILL DO
UGO2PCS	YOU GO TO PIECES
URBRYT1	YOU ARE BRIGHT ONE
URABUM	YOU ARE A BUM
UWILLDO	YOU WILL DO
URMYPIC	YOU ARE MY PICK
URMYPIK	YOU ARE MY PICK

URARIOT	YOU ARE A RIOT
URARYOT	YOU ARE A RIOT
URARYET	YOU ARE A RIOT
URNOHLP	YOU ARE NO HELP
URNOFUN	YOU ARE NO FUN
UR2XCTG	YOU ARE TOO EXCITING
URTAKEN	YOU ARE TAKEN
UCANB12	YOU CAN BE ONE TOO
UALIGOT	YOU ALL I GOT
URABUMR	YOU ARE A BUMMER
URADUDE	YOU ARE A DUDE
UCANCIT	YOU CAN SEE IT
URAWYNR	YOU ARE A WHINNER
URAWINR	YOU ARE A WINNER
URARISK	YOU ARE A RISK
UR2BLVD	YOU ARE TO BE LOVED
URAGTLN	YOU ARE A GENTLEMAN
URANTWT	YOU ARE A KNITWIT
URABORE	YOU ARE A BORE
URABOAR	YOU ARE A BORE
URATWNK	YOU ARE A TWINK
URATWKE	YOU ARE A TWINKIE

"V"

VETSROK	VETERANS ARE OK
VETCAR	VET CAR
VETZCAR	VETERANS CAR
VETZRN1	VETS ARE NUMBER ONE
VETDOC	VET DOCTOR
VACZSUK	VACUUMS SUCK
VACSSUC	VACS SUCK
VRYLKLY	VERY LIKELY
VRYPRSL	VERY PERSONAL
VRYPRVT	VERY PRIVATE
VRYUGLY	VERY UGLY
VULTURE	VULTURE
VULGAR1	VULGAR ONE
VAGRANT	VAGRANT
VALCANO	VALCANO
VELYGUD	ORIENTAL TALK

VAGRUNT	VAGRANT
VACTIME	VACATION TIME
VACTYME	VACATION TIME
VACNTYM	VACATION TIME

"W"

WRLDPCE	WORLD PEACE
WRDPROC	WORD PROCESSOR
WHORIBL	HORRIBLE
WHORU	WHO ARE YOU
WHORYU	WHO ARE YOU
WNRZSKT	WEINERS & SOUERKRAUT
WEAGREE	WE AGREE
WAYMEIN	WEIGH ME IN
WTRMELN	WATERMELON
WEFIXIT	WE FIX IT
WECUR	WE SEE YOU ARE
WESEEUR	WE SEE YOU ARE
WECUR2	WE SEE YOU ARE TOO
WEFLYHI	WE FLY HIGH
WYZGY	WISE GUY
WYZGUY	WISE GUY
WYZGYZR	WISE GUYS ARE

WYZGYSR	WISE GUYS ARE
WYZGYZ2	WISE GUYS TOO
WYZGYS2	WISE GUYS TOO
WEENJOY	WE ENJOY
WENJOY	WE ENJOY
WENJOYU	WE ENJOY YOU
WECAN2	WE CAN TOO
WECANTO	WE CAN TOO
WEFISH	WE FISH
WEHUNT	WE HUNT
WECANDO	WE CAN DO
WETRYIT	WE TRY IT
WETRYD2	WE TRIED TOO
WER4LIF	WE'RE FOR LIFE
WEREU2	WERE YOU TOO
WILDPIG	WILD PIG
WILDHOG	WILD PIG
WILDBOR	WILD BOAR
WEWALK	WE WALK
WEBOTHR	WE BOTH ARE
WETRY	WE TRY
WEFITE2	WE FIGHT TOO
WECANT	WE CAN'T
WECANTB	WE CAN'T BE
WESICK2	WE SICK TOO
WELUVU2	WE LOVE YOU TOO
WER4U	WERE FOR YOU
WERE4U	WERE FOR YOU

WURYOU2	WERE YOU TOO
WURUTO	WERE YOU TOO
WURU2	WERE YOU TOO
WINEOUT	WINEOUT
WINOUT	WINEOUT
WEHAVIT	WE HAVE IT
WURFURU	WERE FOR YOU
WEGOTIT	WE GOT IT
WHYTRY	WHY TRY
WHYTRY2	WHY TRY TOO
WELOVE2	WE LOVE TOO
WECU2	WE SEE YOU TOO
WECUROK	WE SEE YOU ARE OK
WUR4U2	WERE FOR YOU TOO
WAKMEUP	WAKE ME UP
WEDSIGN	WE DESIGN
WEDTALE	WE DETAIL
WEDTAIL	WE DETAIL
WEDZINE	WE DESIGN
WEDZYNE	WE DESIGN
WURYME	WORRY ME
WURYME2	WORRY ME TOO
WORKME2	WORK ME TOO
WURKME2	WORK ME TOO
WRYWART	WORRY WART
WARZOUT	WARS OUT
WORKNUT	WORKNUT
WURKME	WORK ME

VANITY PLATE EXPRESSIONS

WORKME	WORK ME
WURKAHO	WORKAHOLIC
WESUPTU	WE SUPPORT YOU
WILDAXES	WILD AXES
WENEZ2U	WEINIES TO YOU
WEDUE2	WE DO TO
WLYWORM	WOOLY WORM
WLYWURM	WOOLY WORM
WYTZWYT	WHITES WHITE
WNDRBOY	WONDERBOY
WNDRIF	WONDER IF
WUNDRIF	WONDER IF
WINDSOX	WIND SOCKS
WIPTOUT	WIPED OUT
WYPTOUT	WIPED OUT
WHATALN	WHAT A LINE
WUZI2NO	WAS I TO KNOW
WILIT2U	WILL IT TO YOU
WEDUETO	WE DO TOO
WEDEW	WE DO
WEDUE	WE DO
WEDODO	WE DUE DUE
WEDODO2	WE DUE DUE TOO
WIZENUP	WISEN UP
WISEUP	WISE UP
WYSEUP	WISE UP
WYZRWZR	WISE ARE WISER
WOWMOM	SAME BWD & FWD UPSIDE DOWN

WIGLMYN	WIGGLE MINE
WYGLMYN	WIGGLE MINE
WIGLME	WIGGLE ME
WIGLME2	WIGGLE ME TOO
WER24U	WERE TO FOR YOU
WER24YU	WERE TO FOR YOU
WATCHIT	WATCH IT
WTRVANE	WEATHER VANE
WTRMANE	WATER MAIN
WURKZGD	WORKS GOOD
WURKHD	WORK HARD
WURKZHD	WORK HARD
WAREIT	WEAR IT
WERZMYN	WHERE'S MINE
WELZDRY	WELLS DRY
WELZDRI	WELLS DRY
WELZHI	WELLS HIGH
WELDIGR	WELL DIGGER
WEREPDQ	WERE PRETTY DARNED QUICK
WIPEOUT	WIPE OUT
WINGIT	WING IT
WHISKRZ	WHISKERS
WRITEON	RIGHT ON
WOLFHND	WOLF HOUND
WLFITUP	WOLF IT UP
WULFHND	WOLF HOUND
WLFHND	WOLF HOUND
WEJYPTR	WE JIPPED HER

WEGYPTR	WE JIPPED HER
WERWOLF	WERE WOLF
WEREDGO	WHERE DEGO
WAFERME	WAIT FOR ME
WYNDOZE	WINDOWS
WYNZFYN	WINES FINE
WAYTOGO	WAY TO GO
WANDERR	NOMAD
WNTMYBY	WANT MY BODY
WANANEK	WANNA NECK
WANANEC	WANNA NECK
WAFFLEZ	WAFFLES
WETSHTZ	WET T-SHIRTS
WOKTAWK	CHINESE COOKING
WOKTALK	CHINESE COOKING
WOKALON	WALK ALONE
WORK4ME	WORK FOR ME
WOKALNG	WALK ALONG
WATZUPR	WHATS YOUR PROBLEM
WELL2DO	WELL TO DO
WEEKNEZ	WEAK KNEES
WEKNEZ	WEAK KNEES
WILOWE	WILLOW
WILLOW	WILLOW
WLDGESE	WILD GOOSE
WELL2DO	WELL TO DO
WELTODO	WELL TO DO
WELHELD	WELL HEELED

WHINER	WHINER
WHINNEY	WHINNEY
WHISTLE	WHISTLE
WHIPRWL	WHIPPERWILL
WHPRWIL	WHIPPERWILL
WHTGOST	WHITE GHOST
WYFLOVR	WIFE LOVER
WYFLUVR	WIFE LOVER
WASHTUP	WASHED UP
WKAFTWK	WEEK AFTER WEEK
WLDATLV	WILD AT LOVE
WHOTERS	HOOTERS
WHOTERZ	HOOTERS
WACVUZ	WASHINGTON SEA VIEWS
WACVUES	WASHINGTON SEA VIEWS
WALLOPT	WALLOPED
WODNIW	WINDOW BACKWARDS
WHONOSE	WHO KNOWS
WHONOZ	WHO KNOWS
WHONOZE	WHO KNOWS
WUCLOX	WINDUP CLOCKS
WUCLOXZ	WINDUP CLOCKS
WEEKNEE	WEINIE
WNDRWMN	WONDER WOMAN
WYZGALS	WISE GALS
WYZGALS	WISE GALS
WUNBYAL	WON BY ALL
WHOSURE	HOOSIER

WATADOG	WHAT A DOG
WDNSHUZ	WOOKEN SHOES
WYRWEUP	WHY ARE WE UP
WDNHEAD	WOODEN HEAD

"X"

XCUZEME	EXCUSE ME
XCZME	EXCUSE ME
XQUEZME	EXCUSE ME
XCZME2	EXCUSE ME TOO
XCZIT	EXCUSE IT
XQUEZUP	EXCUSE UP
XCYTME	EXCITE ME
XSITEME	EXCITE ME
XITEME	EXCITE ME
XTRMNTR	EXTERMINATOR
XTASEA	ECSTACY
XTASEE	ECSTACY
XTATIC	ECSTATIC
XTRALV	EXTRA LOVE
XTRALUV	EXTRA LOVE
XTRACIT	EXTRACT IT
XPURTS	EXPERTS

XPURTZ	EXPERTS
XPORTS	EXPORTS
XPORTZ	EXPORTS
XTRASHN	EXTRATION
XPRTZR	EXPERTS ARE
XPURTZR	EXPERTS ARE
XPCTME	EXPECT ME
EXPECTME	EXPECT ME
XPCTME2	EXPECT ME TOO
XCUUZME	EXCUSE ME
XCQUZME	EXCUCE ME
XCUZME	EXCUSE ME
XCUSME	EXCUSE ME
XQUSEME	EXCUSE ME
XQQQZME	EXCUSE ME
XTRANYC	EXTRA NICE
XPERTEZ	EXPERTISE
XIBISHN	EXHIBITION
XITEME2	EXCITE ME TOO
XES41EN	ANYONE FOR S_ _ BACKWARDS
XPLODED	EXPLODED
X10DEAD	EXTENDED
X10D2ME	EXTEND TO ME
XPRTEAZ	EXPERTISE
XPRTEZ	EXPERTISE
XPEURTZ	EXPERTISE
XSPURTS	EXPERTS
XRCYZME	EXERCISE ME
XRSYZME	EXERCISE ME

"Y"

YRUTRBL	WHY ARE YOU TROUBLE
YTRYIT	WHY TRY IT
YDOIT	WHY DO IT
YOU2RQT	YOU TWO ARE CUTE
YDOUCIT	WHY DO YOU SEE IT
YSOBLUE	WHY SO BLUE
YSOBLU	WHY SO BLUE
YRUOK	WHY ARE YOU OK
YRWE	WHY ARE WE
YOUTOO	YOU TOO
YDOICU2	WHY DO I SEE YOU TOO
YDOICU	WHY DO I SEE YOU
YBOTHER	WHYBOTHER
YRUMAD	WHY ARE YOU MAD
YRUMIFT	WHY ARE YOU MIFFED
YRSTOGO	YOURS TO GO
YRZTOGO	YOURS TO GO

YRS2GO	YOURS TO GO
YRZ2GO	YOURS TO GO
YOU2IF	YOU TOO IF
YOUR12	YOU ARE ONE TOO
YOU2ARE	YOU TOO ARE
YOU2R	YOU TOO ARE
YOURZRQT	YOURS ARE CUTE
YUBLUIT	YOU BLEW IT
YRUWILD	WHY ARE YOU WILD
Y2RUOK	WHY TO ARE YOU OK
Y2RUBLU	WHY TO ARE YOU BLUE
YDUUDU	WHY DO YOU DO
YDUUDUE	WHY DO YOU DO
YDOUTRY	WHY DO YOU TRY
YNOTTRY	WHY NOT TRY
YKNOTME	WHY NOT ME
YNOTRY1	WHY NOT TRY ONE
YNOTNOW	WHY NOT NOW
YDOWEC	WHY DO WE SEE
YDOWE	WHY DO WE
YDUEWE	WHY DO WE
YDOWEWE	WHY DO WE WEWE
YTRY2	WHY TRY TO
YRTYTWO	WHY TRY TO
YTELLME	WHY TELL ME
YTELME	WHY TELL ME
YOUDEVL	YOU DEVIL
YUDEVIL	YOU DEVIL

YUDEVLU	YOU DEVIL YOU
YBIFUR2	WHY BE IF YOU ARE TO
YBIFUR	WHY BE IF YOU ARE
YCMEIF	WHY SEE ME IF
YZAZME	WISE AS ME
YRUPUNY	WHY ARE YOU PUNY
YDONTU2	WHY DON'T YOU TOO
YRUSOSO	WHY ARE YOU SOSO
YGIVEIN	WHY GIVE IN
YGIVEUP	WHY GIVE UP
YCANTUB	WHY CAN'T YOU BE
YZITSO	WHY'S IT SO
YABUT	YA BUT
YAHBUT	YA BUT
YDOYELL	WHY DO YELL
YDOUYEL	WHY DO YOU YELL
YDOULYE	WHY DO YOU LIE
YDOUULIE	WHY DO YOU LIE
YDUULYE	WHY DO YOU LIE
YDUDLAY	WHY DO YOU DELAY
YURGD4O	WHY YOU ARE GOOD FOR NOTHING
YRZIZQT	YOURS IS CUTE
YDUYUC	WHY DO YOU SEE
YDUYUC1	WHY DO YOU SEE ONE
YDUYUCM	WHY DO YOU SEE'M
YDUYUGO	WHY DO YOU GO
YBABUT	WHY BE A BUTT

VANITY PLATE EXPRESSIONS

YFYTIT	WHY FIGHT IT
YRUINIT	WHY RUIN IT
YRZISTO	YOURS IS TOO
YORSIZ2	YOURS IS TOO
YOUZIS2	YOURS IS TOO
YOURMYN	YOUR MINE
YOUMYNE	YOUR MINE
YURMYN	YOUR MINE
YURMYNE	YOUR MINE
YOURMYN	YOUR MINE
YORMYN	YOUR MINE
YOKZONU	YOKES ON YOU
YZURZ	WHYS YOUR
YROKBYI	YOUR OK BY I
YLEBELY	YELLY BELLY
YRZRMYN	YOURS OR MINE
YZORMYN	YOURS OR MINE
YBCRUEL	WHY BE CRUEL
YZITFIT	WHYS IT FIT
YZITSO	WHYS IT SO
YUZGUYZ	YOU GUYS
YUZGALZ	YOU GALS
YUYZUP	WHY YOU WISE UP
YZUP4ME	WISE UP FOR ME
YDBATET	WHY DEBATE IT
YURZ2C	YOURS TO SEE
WCME2	WHY SEE ME TOO
YCMENOW	WHY SEE ME NOW

YZASME2	WISE AS ME TOO
YZAZME	WISE AS ME
YZAZME2	WISE AS ME TOO
YZASME	WISE AS ME
YDOULUZ	WHY DO YOU LOSE
YABADAB	FLINTSTONE TALK
YURZR2	YOURS ARE TOO
YURZFIT	YOURS FIT
YURZFYT	YOURS FIGHT
YRPRFCT	YOUR PERFECT
YERPSE	OSPREY BACKWARDS
YURUNEK	YOUR UNIQUE
YGROUP	WHY GROW UP
YGROWUP	WHY GROW UP
YNNROZS	WINE N ROSES
YROK4ME	YOUR OK FOR ME
YRUSONC	WHY ARE YOU SO NICE
YDOUSEW	WHY DO YOU SEW
YRZ2EXP	YOURS TO EXPERIENCE
YRNSPNR	YARN SPINNER
YUBOOL	YOU BE COOL
YBATAWL	WHY BE AT ALL
YULCIT2	YOU'LL SEE IT TOO
YRUDEEF	WHY ARE YOU DEEF
YB14ME	WHY BE ONE FOR ME
YB14ME2	WHY BE ONE FOR ME TOO
YRZBYTZ	YOURS BITES
YRZFYTZ	YOURS FIGHTS

YAWLCUM	YOU ALL COME
YACHTZ1	YACHTS NUMBER ONE
YACHT2U	YACHT TO YOU
YUKONIK	YUKON INK
YUNGONE	YOUNG ONE
YOGURT	YOGURT
YR2YUNG	YOUR TOO YOUNG
YNG4EVE	YOUNG FOREVER
YUALBUD	YOU ALL BUDDY
YOFOTAS	YOURS FOR THE ASKING
YORZ2C	YOURS TO SEE
YAWHODE	YAHOOTIE
YURMOVE	YOUR MOVE
YRLSMYG	YOUR LOSS MY GAIN
YRLOMYG	YOUR LOSS MY GAIN
YRUMEAN	WHY ARE YOU MEAN
YRUMEEN	WHY ARE YOU MEAN
YRUSICK	WHY ARE YOU SICK
YURSICK	WHY YOU ARE SICK
YRWEFTG	WHY ARE WE FIGHTING
YCME4IT	WHY SEE ME FOR IT
YCMECRY	WHY SEE ME CRY
YESBUT	YES BUT
YRIT4ME	YOUR IT FOR ME
YOURIT	YOUR IT
YURIT	YOUR IT
Y4GETME	WHY FORGET ME
YFRGTME	WHY FORGET ME

YARDBRD	YARD BIRD
YIPEEEE	YIPEEEE
YIIPEEE	YIPEEEE
YURELAX	WHY YOU RELAX
YRUSAD	WHY ARE YOU SAD
YUERKME	WHY YOU ERK ME
YOURANG	YOU RANG
YURANG	YOU RANG
YLDABTU	WILD ABOUT YOU
YLD4U	WILD FOR YOU
YLD4YOU	WILD FOR YOU
YLD4U2	WILD FOR YOU TOO
YULBSRY	YOU'LL BE SORRY
YRUCYOT	WHY ARE YOU QUIET
YLU2LUV	WHIL YOU TWO LOVE
YRUMINE	WHY ARE YOU MINE
YRUBLEW	WHY ARE YOU BLUE
YRUBLU	WHY ARE YOU BLUE
YRUPTYT	WHY ARE YOU UP TIGHT
YBANNT	WHY BE A NUT
YBAKOOK	WHY BE A KOOK
YBABUTT	WHY BE A BUTT
YBABABY	WHY BE A BABY
YRIRICH	WHY ARE I RICH
YRWEFAT	WHY ARE WE FAT
YRWEHPY	WHY ARE WE HAPPY
YBABOOB	WHY BE A BOOB
YRWEUP	WHY ARE WE UP

YABUGME	YOU BUG ME
YESBUTI	YES BUT I
YESUARE	YES YOU ARE
YESYUAR	YES YOU ARE

"Z"

ZISLAST	"Z" IS LAST
ZISZUST	Z IS ZUST
ZNGRZAR	ZINGERS ARE
ZITZRIT	ZITS ARE IT
ZITZUC	ZITS SUCK
ZITZSUK	ZITS SUCK
ZERO4U	ZERO FOR YOU
ZERO4YU	ZERO FOR YOU
ZERO4UZ	ZERO FOR YOUS
ZEROIZO	ZERO IS ZERO
ZEROZNO	ZEROS NO
ZEROSNO	ZEROS NO
ZSRCOOL	ZEEZ ARE COOL
ZZRCOOL	ZEEZ ARE COOL
ZZRZZS	ZEEZ ARE ZEES
ZOOKENI	ZUCCHINI
ZUKEYNI	ZUCCHINI

ZFEETIC	Z ZEE FEET I SEE
ZS4ZERO	ZEES FOR ZERO
ZSRAMST	ZEES ARE A MUST
ZONKED	ZONKED
ZONKET	ZONKED
ZEALOUS	ZEALOUS
ZIPTUP	ZIPPED UP
ZITITUP	ZIP IT UP
ZIPSOPN	ZIPS OPEN
ZIPZOPN	ZIPS OPEN
ZIPSDWN	ZIPS DOWN
ZIPZDWN	ZIPS DOWN"
ZIPPERS	ZIPPERS
ZIPPERZ	ZIPPERS
ZPZOPEN	ZIPS OPEN
ZPSOPEN	ZIPS OPEN
ZIPULIP	ZIP YOUR LIP
ZROZIN	ZEROS IN
ZEROISO	ZERO IS O

"NUMBERS"

"1"

1DEER1	ONE DEAR ONE
1DEAR1	ONE DEAR ONE
1BIGDOC	ONE BIG DOC
1SWEET1	ONE SWEET ONE
1UGLY1	ONE UGLY ONE
1WYZAS	ONE WISE AS
1STYNKR	ONE STINKER
1BYDFLT	WON BY DEFAULT
12PUNCH	ONE TWO PUNCH
1OUTA3	ONE OUTA THREE
12RADOZ	TWELVE ARE A DOZEN
12RDOZN	TWELVE ARE A DOZEN
144ZGRS	144 IS A GROSS
1SYZBGR	ONE SIZE BIGGER
1IDJACK	ONE-EYED JACK
1EYDJAC	ONE-EYED JACK
1EYDJAK	ONE-EYED JACK

1HYIQ	ONE HIGH IQ
1HIGHIQ	ONE HIGH IQ
1X1EQLV	ONE PLUS ONE EQUALS LOVE
1P1EQLV	ONE PLUS ONE EQUALS LOVE
1QUTLOW	ONE QUART LOW
1LNLY1	ONE LONELY ONE
1LONLY1	ONE LONELY ONE
12LVBLD	ONE TO LOVE BLONDES
1QTRPNR	ONE QUARTER POUNDER
1QTRPDR	ONE QUARTER POUNDER
1BORN2B	ONE BORN TO BE
1BYALL	WON BY ALL
14THMNY	ONE FOR THE MONEY
12PACKR	HALFA RACK
1BYANOZ	WON BY A NOSE
1BYANOS	WON BY A NOSE
1BADOOD	ONE BAD DOOD
1BADUDE	ONE BAD DOOD
14GRINS	ONE FOR GRINS
14PEACE	ONE FOR PEACE

"2"

2OLDTOO	TOO OLD TOO
2OLD2	TOO OLD TOO
2OLDTWO	TOO OLD TOO
2OLKTO	TOO OLD TO
2LOVEIS	TO LOVE IS
2LOVIS	TO LOVE IS
2DULL2	TOO DULL TOO
2LATE2	TOO LATE TOO
2LATETO	TOO LATE TOO
2SICKTO	TOO SICK TO
2SICK2	TOO SICK TO
2BIG2	TOO BIG TO
2TINY2	TOO TINY TO
2FRESH2	TOO FRESH TO
2BRNT2B	TO BE OR NOT TO BE
2BORN2B	TO BE OR NOT TO BE
2BORNOT	TO BE OR NOT

2TUFFTO	TOO TOUGH TO
2TOUGH2	TOO TOUGH TO
2BADUR	TOO BAD YOU ARE
2BADUR2	TOO BAD YOU ARE TO
2LATE2C	TOO LATE TO SEE
2LT2CU	TOO LATE TO SEE YOU
2LAT2CU	TOO LATE TO SEE YOU
2FANCY2	TOO FANCY TO
2SKYNIT	TO SKIN IT
2SKINIT	TO SKIN IT
2UGLY2	TOO UGLY TO
2ATEE	TO A TEE
2OUTA3	TWO OUTA THREE
2GOOD2B	TOO GOOD TO BE
2BCRUEL	TO BE CRUEL
2SHORT2	TOO SHORT TO
2FACED	TWO FACED
2HILT	TO HILT
2LETUSB	TO LET US BE
24GIVEU	TO FORGIVE YOU
24GIVU2	TO FORGIVE YOU TOO
21ANFRE	TWINTY-ONE AND FREE
2UFREE	TO YOU FREE
2YUFREE	TO YOU FREE
2TYMZ2	TWO TIMES TWO
2TIMES2	TWO TIMES TWO
221IZ5	TWO TWO ONE IS FIVE
2IMPRST	TOO IMPRESSED

VANITY PLATE EXPRESSIONS

2WISE4U	TOO WISE FOR YOU
2WYZ4U2	TOO WISE FOR YOU TOO
2LIPME	TULIP ME
2QUARTZ	TWO QUARTS
2QUARTS	HALF GALLON
2X2EQZR	TWO BY TWO EQUALZES
2X4EQZR	TWO BY FOUR EQUALZES
2MIXTUP	TOO MIXED UP
2SAD4U2	TOO SAD FOR YOU TOO
2SAD4YU	TOO SAD FOR YOU
2FEETIC	TWO FEET I SEE
2HT2HNL	TOO HOT TO HANDLE
2HT2HDL	TOO HOT TO HANDLE
2HARD2	TOO HARD TO
2ATLUVR	TO A TEA LOVER
2ATLOVR	TO A TEA LOVER
2BHELD	TO BE HELD
2BDUMPT	TO BE DUMPED
2THREAR	TO THE REAR
2THERER	TO THE REAR
2HOT2	TOO HOT TO
24THSHO	TO FOR THE SHOW
2TYT4ME	TOO TIGHT FOR ME
2U4FREE	TO YOU FOR FREE
2BESOSO	TO BE SOSO
2UWITLV	TO YOU WITH LOVE
2DOWELL	TO DO WELL
2DABANK	TO DA BANK

2DASTOR	TO DA STORE
2DAPOOL	TO DA POOL
2DADOC	TO DA DOCK
2DAOFIC	TO DA OFFICE
2DAOFIS	TO DA OFFICE
2B1ASK	TO BE ONE ASK
2FTLONG	TWO FOOT LONG
2SANARZ	TUCSON, ARIZONA
2BAD4U	TOO BAD FOR YOU
2BAD4YU	TOO BAD FOR YOU
2NOMEIS	TO KNOW ME IS
2NOMEIZ	TO KNOW ME IS
2TF2HDL	TOO TOUGH TO HANDLE
2ASFRSH	TWICE AS FRESH
2AZFRSH	TWICE AS FRESH
2PURDAY	TWO PER DAY
2PERDAY	TWO PER DAY
2BSOBER	TO BE SOBER
2BUKZ4U	TWO BUCKS FOR YOU
2BCREWL	TO BE CRUEL
2BCUDLD	TO BE CUDDLED
2BACTOR	TO BE ACTOR
24PROF1	TWO FOR PRICE OF ONE
2BMARYD	TO BE MARRIED
2WKNEES	TWO WEAK KNEES
2WKNEEZ	TWO WEAK KNEES
221ODDS	TWO TO ONE ODDS
2FERONE	TWO FOR ONE

2FERWON	TWO FOR ONE
2FURONE	TWO FOR ONE
2FURWON	TWO FOR ONE
2OFU4ME	TWO OF YOU FOR ME
2YLD4ME	TOO WILD FOR ME
2WILD4U	TOO WILD FOR ME
2B4SURE	TO BE FOR SURE
2NYTIDO	TO NIGHT I DO
2NYTUDO	TO NIGHT YOU DO
2NOMEIS	TO KNOW ME IS
2NOMEIZ	TO KNOW ME IS
2BXPCTD	TO BE EXPECTED

"3"

3ZCROWD	THREE'S A CROWD
32GTRDY	THREE TO GET READY
36ZRPRF	36'S ARE PERFECT
3IZMANY	THREE IS MANY
3ISMANY	THREE IS MANY
3ISMENY	THREE IS MANY
3IZMENY	THREE IS MANY
3ZTRUBL	THEREE'S TROUBLE
3STEWGZ	THREE STOOGES
3STOOGZ	THREE STOOGES
33ZRNYN	THREE THREES ARE NINE
33IR9	THREE THREE ARE NINE

"4"

4URONGD	FOR YOUR OWN GOOD
4MSTLYU	FOR MOSTLY YOU
4SFULL	FORCEFUL
4CINIT	FORESEE IN IT
4CITOUT	FORESEE IT OUT
4CEPTZ	FORCEPS
4CPTZ	FORCEPS
4EVR4ME	FOREVER FOR ME
4EVRMOR	FOREVER MORE
4SITE	FORESIGHT
4SIGHT	FORESIGHT
4CHUNS	FORTUNES
4CHUNZ	FORTUNES
4GETIT	FORGET IT
4GET2	FORGET TO
4MYBODY	FOR MY BODY
4CLOSUR	FORECLOSURE

4GRANTD	FOR GRANTED
4CLOZUR	FORECLOSURE
4GOTYOU	FORGOT YOU
4GOTU	FORGOT YOU
4GOTU2	FORGOT YOU TOO
4SITEOF	FORESIGHT OF
4SITEOV	FORESIGHT OF
4JUSTUS	FOR JUSTICE
4JUSTIS	FOR JUSTICE
4SKYNZ2	FOR SKINS TOO
421IZ7	FOR TWO ONE IS SEVEN
4FLUSHR	FOREFLUSHER
4U2USET	FOR YOUTO USE IT
4CANS4U	FOUR CANS FOR YOU
4CANZ4U	FOUR CANS FOR YOU
4U2CME	FOR YOU TO SEE ME
4U2CFRE	FOR YOU TO SEE FREE
4MULA	FORMULA
42OFUS	FOR TWO OF US
4KDSSAK	FOR KIDS SAKE
4KDZSAK	FOR KIDS SAKE
4UIHOWL	FOR YOU I HOWL
42NIGHT	FOR TONIGHT
4TNIGHT	FOR TONIGHT
4LFOFME	FOR LIFE OF ME
4WHLRZ	FOUR WHEELERS
4WHLZGR	FOUR WHEELS GREAT
42TYMRZ	FOR TWO TIMERS
4MONEY2	FOR MONEY TOO

4CFUTUR	FORESEE FUTURE
4FREE2U	FOR FREE TO YOU
4INSTNC	FOR INSTANCE
4HYSKYZ	FOR HIGH SKIES
4SALBYOW	FOR SALE BY OWNER
4U2UZIT	FOR YOU TO USE IT
4YURLOV	FOR YOUR LOVE
4URLOVE	FOR YOUR LOVE
4ALOFYU	FOR ALL OF YOU
4SQUARE	FOUR SQUARE
4ULUZRS	FOR YOU LOSERS
4ULUZRZ	FOR YOU LOSERS
4ULUSRS	FOR YOU LOSERS
4HAND	FOREHAND
4U2NJOY	FOR YOU TO ENJOY
4UONLY	FOR YOU ONLY
4EVRMOR	FOREVER MORE
4HELRHW	FOR HELL OR HIGH WATER
4GRINS	FOR GRINS
4GRINZ	FOR GRINS
4U2CUS	FOR YOU TO SEE US
4U2CME	FOR YOU TO SEE ME
4URGOOD	FOR YOUR GOOD
4URSAKE	FOR YOUR SAKE
4ENMAID	FOREIGN MADE
4NMAYD	FOREIGN MADE
4NMAYDN	FOREIGN MAIDEN
4URHELP	FOR YOUR HELP
4NSTNC	FOR INSTANCE

"5"

501BUNZ   501JEANS
5WHLOVR   5HE WHEEL LOVER

"6"

6ISSEXY	SIX IS SEXY
6IZSEXY	SIX IS SEXY
6RHLFDZ	SIX ARE HALF DOZEN
6PACKER	SIX PACKER

"7"

7CUMA11	SEVEN COME A ELEVEN
7CUMZ11	SEVEN COMES ELEVEN
7DAZAWK	SEVEN DAYS A WEEK
7LTLPGS	SEVEN LITTLE PIGS
7LTLPGZ	SEVEN LITTLE PIGS

"8"

8OCLKRK	EIGHT OCLOCK ROCK
8BALLZ	EIGHT BALLS
8BALZ	EIGHT BALLS
8BALZOK	EIGHT BALLS OK

"9"

9ZNICE	NINES NICE
9ZNYCR	NINES NICER
9ZNYCE	NINES NICE
9ZRNEAT	NINES ARE NEAT
9ZRNICE	NINES ARE NEAT
90GDWIL	90 GOODWILL GAMES

"10"

10DERLV	TENDER LOVE
102YRBZ	TEND TO YOUR BUSINESS
10DER1	TENDER ONE
102PZQZ	TEND TO YOUR PZ & QZ
10NISS	TENNIS
102UBIZ	TEND TO YOUR BUSINESS
10CITY	TENSITY

"0"

0IZNONE	ZERO IS NONE
0IZNUTG	ZERO IS NUTTING
0ZOUGHT	ZERO'S OUGHT
0IZ0	ZERO IS ZERO
0ISNONE	ZERO IS NONE
0IZNONE	ZERO IS NONE
0ISNUN	ZERO IS NONE
0IZNUN	ZERO IS NONE

Lightning Source UK Ltd.
Milton Keynes UK
UKOW05f1921170317
296920UK00024B/583/P